D1478202

MORE THAN JUST A HOUSE

More Than Just a House: At Home with Collectors and Creators

First published in the United States of America in 2020 by
Rizzoli International Publications, Inc.
300 Park Avenue South
New York, NY 10010
www.rizzoliusa.com

Design - Studio Frith
Headline Typeface - Studio Frith

Publisher: Charles Miers
Editor: Giulia Di Filippo
Copyeditor: Linda Schofield
Production manager: Alyn Evans

2020 2021 2022 2023 2024 / 10 9 8 7 6 5 4 3 2 1

Distributed in the U.S. trade by Random House, New York

Printed in China

ISBN-13: 978-0-8478- 6771-4

Library of Congress Control Number: 2020933260

Visit us online:
Facebook.com/RizzoliNewYork
Twitter: @Rizzoli_Books
Instagram.com/RizzoliBooks
Pinterest.com/RizzoliBooks
Youtube.com/user/RizzoliNY
Issuu.com/Rizzoli

MORE THAN JUST A HOUSE

AT HOME WITH COLLECTORS AND CREATORS

ALEX EAGLE

Photography by Kate Martin
Text by Tish Wrigley

New York · Paris · London · Milan

STEFAN
SIMCHOWITZ

ALEX EAGLE

INTRODUCTION

This book was born from a feeling I often have when I am welcomed into a friend's fabulous house. I look around and wish I could record my experience: not just the color of the walls or the art in the hallway, but the spirit of the place, the way the energy of the person who lives there is expressed in its singular style. I wanted to build a portrait of the best interiors of the moment, filled with the personalities of the brilliant people who live there.

More Than Just a House belongs to F. Scott Fitzgerald, being the title of his dark Jazz Age fairy tale centered around a crumbling mansion in the American South. The two books are very different, but I like to think mine shares Fitzgerald's idea that houses are more than walls and decoration, that they are given life and relevance by the people who live there.

Some of the contributors I have known all my life, a few are my friends' friends, many I have met through Instagram. It is a reflection of the modern network, individuals brought together across time and distance through technology and its awesome capacity to create connections. One common thread is that they inspire me—what they do and how they do it, the way they design, create, and live. At the heart of the matter is that we are all collectors.

I have been collecting since I was a child. It started off with small things—thimbles, stamps, postcards, each a joyful find to be treasured individually and as one of many.

Getting older, I honed my eye. My attention turned to fashion, furniture, art, and objects: pieces from Martin Margiela's tenure at Hermès, Japanese ceramics, art books, work by Irving Penn, mid-century modern furniture. I still remember catching sight of a George Nakashima chair in Les Puces in Paris and being left speechless. I hadn't heard of Nakashima

FM
FINE TUNING
FULL AUTO STOP
MEMORY — ON COUNTER
JVC

before, but discovering that piece made me start researching him, learning everything I could about his work, seeking out more of his furniture for my house.

Collections can start in a single moment with a single object. Collections can be inherited—heirlooms passed down through generations that tell the story of a family. Pieces can be sourced through antique dealers or auction houses, alerts on eBay or accidental finds at flea markets. Priceless treasures have cost the earth or been picked up for a song.

In these pages we have foregrounded not just the people but their favorite things. It was a joy to discover Kim Jones's passion for the Bloomsbury Group, walk through Indrė Šerpytytė's house full of art by women, meet Marie-Louise Sciò's family of pelicans that give her famous hotel its name, see Rosa de la Cruz's cluster of Chris Ofili's *Afromuses*, and experience Ulysses de Santi's peerless array of Brazilian modern design.

As the world evolves, jobs change, and technology redraws the boundaries between work and family life, I am fascinated to see how creatives have adapted their homes to reflect a new reality, some by turning where they live into incubators for their ideas, others by keeping the lines between office and home life unblurred.

Each house is unique. From a prefab in upstate New York to a stately home in the Tuscan hillside, from a former president's residence to a Marrakech *riad*, they span continents and cultures, ranging from big to small, lavish to minimalist, historic to contemporary.

Every home gave me something, be it a paint color, a new artist, a brand of tea, the name of an antiques store, or a novel way of seeing the world. Making this book, I realized that interiors are the bones of a house, but the people, their objects, and their collections are the souls.

BIANCA ARRIVABENE

The Arrivabene family has lived in Venice's Palazzo Papadopoli for two centuries, witness to the city's unchanging beauty and ever-growing influx of visitors. The palazzo's current owners are Giberto and Bianca, who moved in soon after their marriage in 1988 and raised their family of five children in the eaves.

"When we got there, there was nothing, no decor–just a beautiful pigment on the wall and these extraordinary beams," remembers Bianca. "The beams run the whole width of the house and were made from trees that were cut down in the Dolomites, and floated all the way downriver into the lagoon to build Venice's palazzos."

Inheriting a sixteenth-century palazzo as newlyweds in their twenties was a formidable proposition. At the time, most of the building was taken up with offices, including the ministry for schooling in Venice. "We'd have all the teachers in there, striking," Bianca recalls. "They would sit on the stairs and write on the walls; the house was a mess."

In 2005 the offices started to move on and the Arrivabenes got a mortgage, renovated the piano nobile with their bare hands, and began renting it out. "We managed to get amazing projects– Marco Tullio Giordana's film *Sanguepazzo* was shot here, we had the Ukrainian pavilion for four biennales in a row, Robert Polidori shot a Bottega Veneta campaign. We met amazing people and had a lot of fun."

In 2007 Bianca's husband met with the founder of the Aman Hotels, Adrian Zecha. "He told Giberto he wanted to rent it, and my husband said, 'But there's a problem, we are not leaving.' And Adrian said, 'My guests will be delighted to meet you.'"

The financial crisis delayed the project, but the Aman Venice has been open since 2013 and is considered the best hotel in the city. For Bianca, it has been a dream come true. "We are so happy, it is the most important project of our life and we have managed to move it into a safer place. Today the house is fit for another 500 years."

E IO
PAGO!

Their two-story abode in the attic remains very similar to how it was when they first moved in thirty years ago. "My husband did all the downstairs—he has very good taste—and I did all the upstairs where the children were. We have not bought any furniture. What was in the house when we arrived, we used." The two floors are packed with art, sculpture, photographs, furniture, fabrics, and books. Every surface tells a story, be it a family tree,

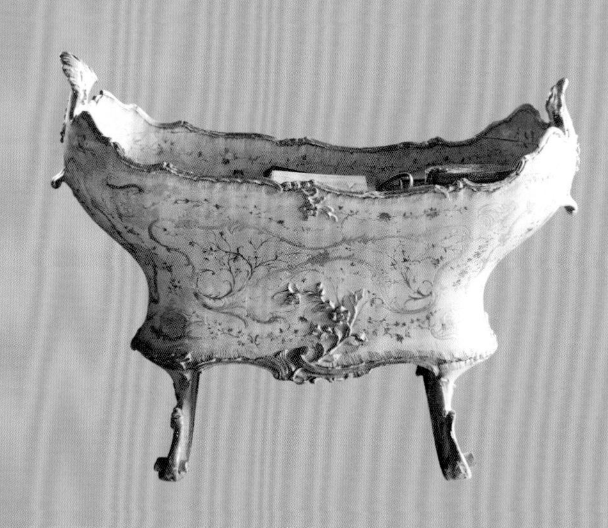

a boat in full sail on a gilded table, Bianca's collection of passport photos filched from her children's wallets, clusters of silver cups, works in glass by Giberto, or a cast of a child's head sporting a moped helmet. "When you're young, you just do things," she shrugs. "There's no overthinking. The house is very relaxed. There's everything—contemporary photography, a portrait of Giberto's granny, a box that came from India, a candle that we found in a market, and the furniture is a mixture of what came. I sometimes buy new things, but already the house is so full. There are days when I want to get rid of everything and be minimal, but I don't think that could ever happen." Bianca's world is Venice. As deputy chairman of Christie's Italy, her schedule is packed, but she also runs an events company and oversees Giberto's Murano

glass design business. "I love traveling, but I have my rhythms in Venice. I love my routine. It is the best lifestyle on earth. You have the good weather, the best-quality food in the market and the restaurant. People have big smiles because of the sun and the good tomatoes. Then there's the beauty. Everything is beautiful."

This beauty has drawn a nearly unmanageable number of tourists to Venice, and Bianca has been a firsthand witness to how this has affected her city. "What is disappearing is life—schools, children, the tiny supermarket, the grocery, they are closing. But when people say we need to create regulations, the first thing they say is no hotels, and we obviously have done a hotel so I'm in a difficult situation." All Bianca's children have now flown the nest, her elder daughters living in Milan, her younger children at school and university abroad, but they are back all the time. "I think we have managed to create what one would call home. I don't know how exactly but it happened. It's about heart, and how you spend time together and how you get those conversations—good, bad, crying, laughing—in one place. The place where you have done all of that, that's home."

L'HERITIER-GUYOT
CRÈME DE CASSIS DE DIJON

SERPENTINE
VITRA
NOTRE
ALASKA ALASKA
S.R. STUDIO C/O ALASKA ALASKA
BRAUN
180 STRAND
EM PTY STRAND
HANS-ULRICH OBRIST
& SKEPTA

TAWANDA CHIWESHE

Traditional wisdom dictates that office spaces are designed differently from domestic spaces, with contradictory priorities in mind. Where one is for work, the other is for sanctuary; where one is a thoroughfare of people, the other is a retreat from the world.

Tawanda Chiweshe, designer and studio director at Alaska Alaska™ c/o Virgil Abloh, does not see those distinctions. His office, housed within brutalist London landmark 180 The Strand, may not bear a physical similarity to his home in Whitechapel, but the aesthetic aligns.

"They are similar in that their design has been a process of accumulation," he says. "With both, I take a curatorial approach, bringing in pieces and seeing how time allows something you have in your life to change in terms of where it sits—in your head, in your heart, or on your shelf."

Born in Harare, Zimbabwe, Chiweshe moved to the UK with his family when he was six, settling in Hertfordshire. Having studied product design at Central Saint Martins in 2016, he was completing an internship at Carpenters Workshop Gallery in Mayfair when he got wind of a Virgil Abloh furniture project that was taking shape. "I sent Virgil an e-mail and he replied the day later. Knowing what I now know about the volume of e-mail he gets, I can't believe that he got it, read it, and answered. It was a triple whammy of luck."

Chicago-based Abloh makes a strong case for being the twenty-first century's definitive Renaissance man. As artistic director of Louis Vuitton menswear, CEO of personal line Off-White, architect, artist, DJ, and Kanye West collaborator, his output extends across the world and almost every creative practice.

But Alaska Alaska™ holds a unique place in his extensive roster. Chiweshe explains, "Our projects are basically everything Virgil does outside of fashion. Alaska Alaska™ is solely his, and we work with him on everything he wants. Essentially we are an ideation hub that is for Virgil alone."

Chiweshe's office has an unvarnished feel, with its untreated floors, stark white walls, and windows looking out onto an always-shifting London. "We want to allow time to grow," he says. "The Strand is brutalist and it's a blank canvas inside, so that's how we've approached the studio as well, so that it does mirror where we are in time and space." Most pertinently, what is represented within the walls are Alaska Alaska™ projects past and present. "Whether we are doing an installation or a sculpture or a product, the studio becomes an accumulation of stuff that has had a role within the process of making and discovery. It's always interesting the dialogue that forms because you're taking objects from different spaces, different rationales, different contexts altogether and when they come together in the studio, they begin to communicate with one another." Pieces include a Vitra prototype chair, reimagined by the studio in bright orange with an acrylic frame, a trainer from Abloh's first collaboration with Nike, and a gray Max Lamb chair from an activation in Stockholm that invited people to use standardized timber to create their own iconic piece of design.

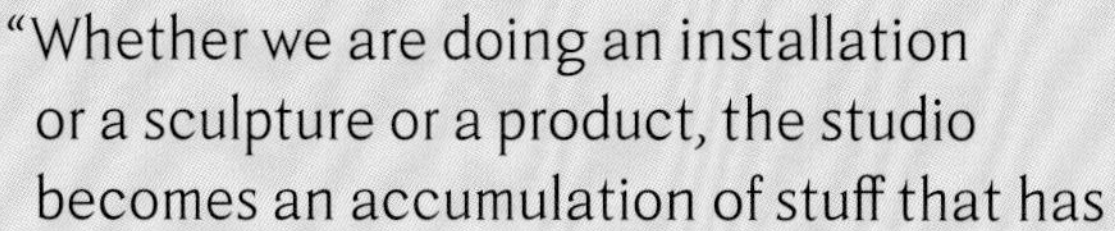

This is KILIMANJARO no.11
Featuring: Marina Abramovic,
AA Bronson, Martin Creed,
Wangechi Mutu, Laure Prouvost
and Charles Ray — Body of Art
ISSN 14791404
Kilimanjaro Autumn/ Winter 2010
kilimag.com
£15.00
evian
ACTIVATE MOVEMENT

morrisroe

"Public engagement is a sentiment we like playing with in the studio," says Chiweshe. "Obviously, we often create exclusive limited-edition items, but we like to engage with the idea of allowing access into the design. Virgil is always playing around with the idea of what he calls 'the purist and the tourist.' Who does this project speak to? And where do we have the opportunity to speak to several voices at once?" Looking around the studio makes it clear that each item has contributed to feeding the minds of Abloh, Chiweshe and

their team, and, for Chiweshe, this is a sentiment he lives with at home too. "I collect stuff that I've contributed towards," he says. "There's something very interesting about creating something from scratch and then seeing it come to exist in the world over time. As a kid I used to think that when you took a photo of someone, part of them was absorbed into the picture, and for me a product works in a similar way. The time spent creating something is very much inherent in the thing. So for me the personal objects that I collect are the things I've been involved in making."

ALGERIA
EGYPT
SAUDI
ARABIA
FRENCH SUDAN
FRENCH WEST AFRICA
ANGLO-EGYPTIAN
SUDAN
ETHIOPIA
KENYA
BELGIAN
CONGO
TANGANYIKA
NORTHERN
SOUTHERN
RHODESIA
Bombay
ARABIAN
Recife
São Paulo
Rio de Janeiro
45
75

Karina Deyko & David de Rothschild

Karina Deyko and her boyfriend, David de Rothschild, have been in their Venice Beach house since 2010. "Basically it's like a compound," says Deyko. "It's a group of studios around a shared courtyard that was owned by the late photographer Guy Webster. Ten years ago we sublet one studio, and now we own three."

The draw of the lofty, light-filled spaces is not hard to see, but for Deyko it was a big transition. "I used to live in Echo Park and had very much chosen to be an East LA person, but David said if he was going to live in LA it had to be by the beach. Psychologically, it was hard to move west, but once I was here I loved it. You can walk everywhere, there are so many artists and creatives, and all the best restaurants are here."

Formerly a mechanic's shop—a faded Texaco sign is still visible above the door—the space has transformed organically, with Deyko and de Rothschild taking their time, layering it with memories from their eleven years together. "I've definitely grown up here, and when you grow up in a place it represents so many parts of you," says Deyko.

The couple met at Burning Man—they go back every year to celebrate their anniversary—while de Rothschild was immersed in creating the Plastiki, the 60-foot catamaran made out of 12,500 reclaimed plastic bottles that he sailed from San Francisco to Sydney to raise awareness of environmental issues including climate change. Today, from one of the Venice studios he runs Lost Explorer, an eco-minded lifestyle brand.

"David's work space is separate but very much there. When I feel like I need my space I stay in, but then when I come out I'm just hit with this

creative energy. There is always someone coming over, someone to talk to, to order food with, watch a movie on the projector. There is so much energy in general."

Deyko, an actress, enjoys living at arm's length from the traditional industry haunts. "I love being in Venice because it takes you outside of the business of being an actress. I love the craft of acting, I don't love the movie business. It's very refreshing to know that it's over there, in Hollywood, and I'm here." Deyko took the lead on the interiors of their home. "We didn't work

VENICE

BEACH

6BKD132

with an interior designer, I worked with a friend of David's who built the Plastiki. We drew it together on a piece of paper, and got a builder to put stuff in. With the white walls it does feel like a blank canvas, which means you can move things around. The things that attract me are different textures, that's what I collect, so I went and found old vintage doors. I love old scaffolding because it's got that beautiful patina, but it's an inexpensive material so you can build cabinets, floors, anything with it."

Clean white walls, reclaimed wood, glass, and greenery dominate, and every item has meaning. "A lot of the art is by our friends, people like Oliver Clegg and Brock Davis, while the little objects are David's from his travels. The map was hanging in Pier 31, where he was building the Plastiki. The spears are from Kenya when we went together. There's a drum I bought him to take to Burning Man that we now use as a coffee table. He likes mapping out his past through all the pieces he's collected. Almost too much. He's definitely a hoarder."

While Los Angeles is officially their home, the couple is nomadic, heading to the UK for the summer, and now they have a baby, spending months at a time in their Malibu beach house. "It's a different feel to LA," says Deyko. "It's a community where everyone drives golf buggies and you all know each other. Everyone's a surfer, a director, or some type of artist, or an old California type who has been there for forty years. It's really sweet."

Another new project is an old school bus David bought just as the couple was getting together. "When we first took it for a drive, the suspension fell out," remembers Deyko, "so we decided to electrify it. Now, eleven years later, the mechanics are done so all that's left to do are the interiors. It will be ready for next year, I hope. We could drive it to South America. That's the plan. When we first met we said, let's have twenty kids and live on the road. Eleven years later, just one kid, but we still want to explore."

STANLEY
PowerLock
25'

MARKHAM ROBERTS
AZUCENA
JARDINS DES ALPES
VIVRE EN ARGENTINE
Giardini & Giardini
NOMAD
SIMONE RUCELLAI
ESCAPE HOTEL STORIES
Ernst Haeckel
EXTREME BEAUTY IN VOGUE
HORST
CALDER | PROUVÉ

MARTINA MONDADORI

An English friend of Martina Mondadori's walked into her Chelsea town house soon after she had first painted the walls and announced, "Oh, you're just so Italian."

"It's true," she shrugs. "It's in my DNA. Growing up in Italy makes you brave with warm colors."

The founder of *Cabana* magazine, Mondadori has made a career of celebrating the best in lustrous, textured, vivid design, and she celebrates the same aesthetic in her own house. The drawing room is painted a rich terracotta, the dining room has accents in Pompeii red, and saffron yellow lines the halls.

Since she grew up in her mother's Renzo Mongiardino-designed apartment in Milan, it might have been a jolt to make the move from Milan to London's chillier climes and neutral interiors. But no. "I was very happy to come," Mondadori says. "Apart from six months in New York in my twenties, I had always lived in Milan. That's where I was born, where I was raised. It was exciting to live somewhere new."

The Chelsea location helped buffer the move—"I love having the butcher, the grocery shop, the newsstand. It's what resonates with Italian people—the village life. And then when I saw this house, I could see my kids doing their homework in the conservatory. I just fell in love."

Mondadori is eloquent on both the origins and evolution of her style. "I have a very specific palette, it's earthy colors, full colors, it came from my mother and what I grew up with. But at the same time, as Italians, we're not proud about our history, we're always trying to be modern in some way, whereas the English really embrace their traditions and history. That's what I've learned from being here. Be proud of your country and embrace it. I'm not sure I would have done what I've done if I'd been in Milan."

It's true that while she has many Italian pieces—a Gio Ponti credenza, an Alighiero Boetti embroidery, Ingo Maurer lamps sourced at Milan Design Fair—her house speaks to a multiplicity of influences. Her sitting room sofa and chairs are upholstered in Persian and African fabrics, a pair of wicker

Redout

stools hail from Morocco, while pieces on the shelves range from a series of Native American playing cards—"they are so familiar, like Italian Scopa cards"—to watercolors by the set designer Lila de Nobili. "I am inspired by things that make me travel with my mind," she says. "I like mixing high and low, pieces that belonged to my father, for example, next to flea market finds, or pieces I've fallen in love with. I particularly love ceramics. They are quintessentially

practical, beautiful, and not necessarily hugely valuable." Her father is commemorated in many of her favorite objects, two fragments of ancient mosaics that hang in the sitting room, as well as works on paper by Edgar Degas and Francisco Goya—"My father was a very eclectic collector, my mother was more about decor. My obsession with laying a table came from my mum. She was always entertaining in our house and involved me very early on." The house is clearly made for entertaining; the large dining table

happily seats twelve and is usually laid with the distinctive Cabana tableware that is Mondadori's most recent endeavor.

"This room is very much the inspiration for the Cabana textiles," Mondadori says. Overseeing the table are clusters of works by Allan McCollum and William Kentridge, as well as a mirror by Marian McEvoy that Mondadori commissioned via Instagram.

"I have always been consistent in my taste," Mondadori says. "But living in England has had a huge impact. For the first year I was here, I wasn't working, I was a new mum, doing up my house, and I spent my time going to museums, visiting historical houses, and creating huge mood boards with things I loved—Italian interiors, English interiors, works of art, and bits and pieces. And I looked at them and thought there is something in here. That's how Cabana was born and how this house was created. Both are about telling an authentic story."

SOILED TOWELS ONLY
PLEASE!
INSTALL TOILET PAPER IN PROPER OVERHAND FASHION
EQUIPMENT
CLEAN TOWELS ONLY
PROTECTIVE CLOTHING
TOWARD CUSTOMER
DETONATOR

Arthur Kar lives in Paris, but do not call him a Parisian.

"In Paris, the answer is always no," he says. "You cannot drive, people are always rude, many of them are jealous. It's motivating, because when I leave Paris, I see how much easier it is to live everywhere else."

Kar has lived in the French capital since he was eight, when his family moved from Lebanon. "I grew up here and I have my business here and I cannot turn my back on Paris because I respect and I like it like this and I have got used to it," he says, "but one thing I don't like to say is that I'm a Parisian."

His business is L'Art de L'Automobile, a dealership for rare, classic cars that has expanded to include an eponymous fashion line inspired by car culture and Kar's interest in art and style.

"I don't consider myself an artist, but I do a job that I consider to be art," he says. "I think it's beautiful to see how things are built, and when you watch them getting built, this is how you know if you want to be a part of it or not."

Parisian or not, Kar now has a new base in the city, an apartment that took four years to find. "Like everything in Paris it's complicated," he says. It was the light and the simplicity that decided it for him. It is painted white throughout, and the only architectural flourishes are the unobtrusive ceiling cornices and herringbone parquet floors.

"I want a house that looks like me," says Kar, "where I've put what I like for myself on the walls rather than things that make it look like a group or personality I can't be. I'd rather have my walls without art if nothing makes me happy. For me the most expensive art is not the best. It's the art that talks to you, touches you somewhere. Those are the pieces, no matter the price."

Kar's great friend Virgil Abloh is a significant presence, from a "Wet Grass" rug and graffitied bench to an orange Vitra brick and Nike Air trainers. Tom Sachs illustrations are clustered in one curved corner, while a John Baldessari nose hangs between the bookshelves and two KAWS x Hajime Sorayama sculptures peek out from behind a red Pierre Jeanneret chair.

"The art I have in my house is cool art, and it's easy to look at and understand. I like art that expresses something, so every time you see it, you learn. These things talk to me and they are part of my life." Evidence of Kar's automobile passion is everywhere, from the car models on bookshelves to a circular rug featuring the logo of his business that features a Volkswagen Golf. "That car is personal," he says. "It's the car I grew up with and so

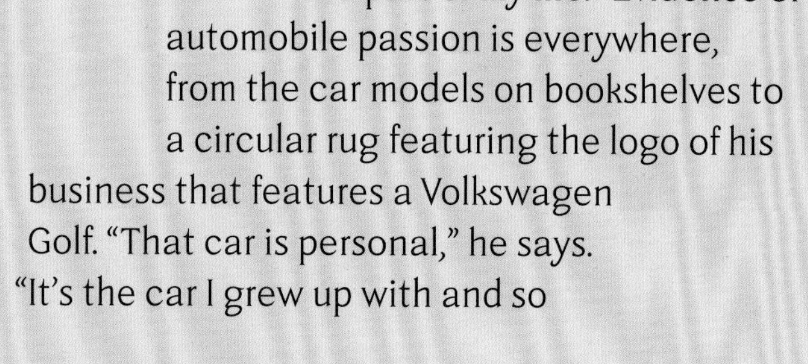

LE CORBUSIER
LE GRAND
KARFOOT
TAMIYA
PIZZA PIZZA
McDONALD'S GRAPHIC STANDARDS
BATMAN NO MAN'S LAND
GEORGE CONDO
CHARLOTTE PERRIAND
FAST
V-VA-691

L'ART DE L'AUTOMOBILE
BENZIN
ESSENCE
GARAGE
MECANIQUE
Kunst am Automobil
Automobile Art
ICE CREAM
NIKE
#54
new balance
WET GRASS.

everything comes from there. I respect people who built their own style on their own experience. This is what I try and do with my company and my designs. I take something that happened or something I saw and I get

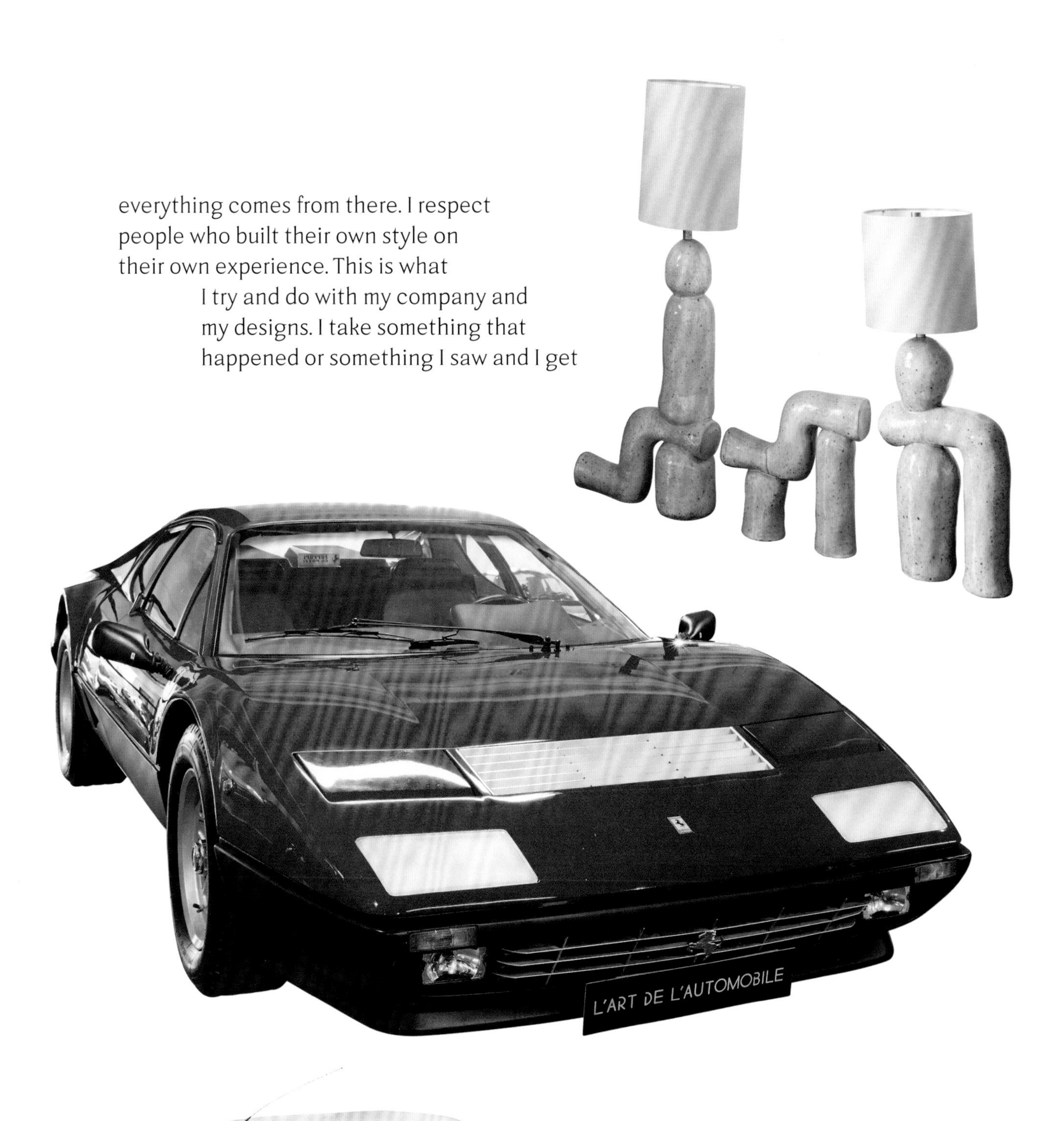

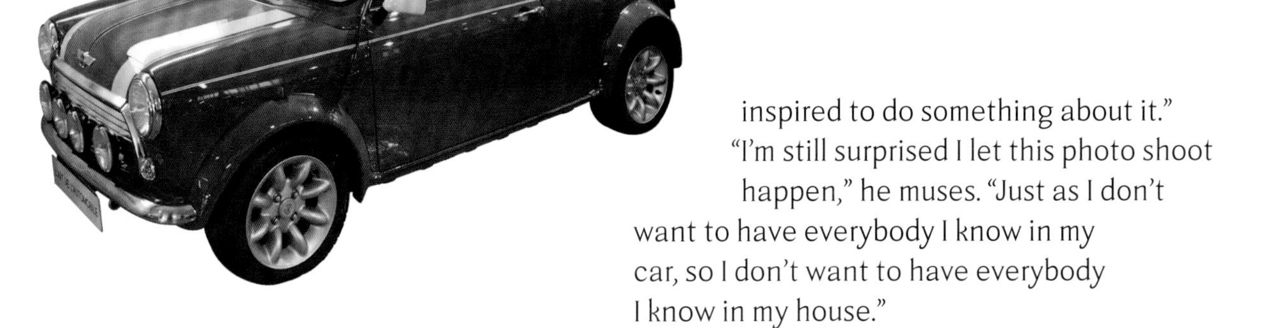

inspired to do something about it."

"I'm still surprised I let this photo shoot happen," he muses. "Just as I don't want to have everybody I know in my car, so I don't want to have everybody I know in my house."

KARFOOT
KARFOOT
KARFOOT
KARFOOT
TAMIYA
SPECIAL TYRE
SPECIAL TYRE
SyncRo
KYOSHO

NOT FOR
RESALE
blonde

THE
NORTH
FACE

John McIlwee & Bill Damaschke

John McIlwee and Bill Damaschke are no strangers to historic houses. The two entertainment executives' main abode is John Lautner's Garcia House in Los Angeles, which they bought as a near-wreck from Vincent Gallo in 2002, but "iconic" was not top of the list when they were looking for a weekend house in the desert.

Indeed, they had ruled out Rancho Mirage—an area east of Palm Springs—as being totally wrong for them. "Big streets, a bunch of rich people, golf courses," summarizes McIlwee. However, when President Gerald and Betty Ford's house came on the market in 2012, they were intrigued.

Built on land given to the couple by their neighbor, Ambassador Leonard Firestone, after Ford's defeat in the 1976 presidential election, the house was designed by noted architect Welton Becket, and the Fords lived there until Betty's death in 2011.

The house itself, its inimitable design as well as its heritage, proved irresistible. "At that time Rancho Mirage was one of the cultural centers of America," says McIlwee. "Bob Hope was there, the Firestones were there, the Annenbergs had Sunnylands nearby. Not only was architecture happening but a real cultural moment for society."

Buying the house was one thing, but deciding how to update it was quite different. "You have to honor the people who built the house, their original vision," says McIlwee. "The Betty Ford house was original, it just wasn't very good. It was Welton Becket who designed it, whose stuff is amazing, but the Fords were very frugal people so the surfaces were very cheap. In the end we chose to make it the best version of what it could be." Collaborating with the architecture firm Marmol Radziner and interior designer Darren Brown, the couple

set about tactfully reconstructing the house, keeping the layout and many design features that the Fords would recognize, while staying true to the taste of McIlwee and Damaschke themselves. "You have to be respectful of something that is original, of the original aesthetic, while not losing sight of what makes sense now," explains McIlwee. "The architecture itself becomes a canvas you can build on, but at the same time it's our house, we're living there, and we had to work out what makes the thing livable to us." McIlwee and Damaschke were firm that nothing should be destroyed unnecessarily.

So while the cheap surfaces and Betty's pink bathroom suite were discarded, other elements were repurposed. The former living room curtains found new life as a guestroom headboard, the bulbs from Betty's vanity mirror now form a dramatic light fixture above the master bed, and the shelves from Jerry's trophy cupboard became a bed frame. Betty Ford's portrait, commissioned by Nelson Rockefeller, now sits in the hall. The dining room has been kept wholly intact, from its original hand-painted leafy mural by Garth Benton to its latticed chairs and lime green carpet, and was the cause of much debate.

"Everyone wanted us to get rid of it. And we said, why? Everything else in the house was worn or ruined, but the dining room was perfect. We're not people who want to live in a weird time capsule of the seventies, but when you think about it, Henry Kissinger was there, the Rockefellers ate dinner there, Bob Hope ate dinner there, why would I get rid of that?"

Both McIlwee and Damaschke are passionate art collectors: "We buy art based on life, and we'll then figure out where it will go," says McIlwee. The house is dotted with pieces by the likes of Patrick Nagel and Dashiell Manley.

"One of our favorite works is by Kirsten Everberg, who did a series called the White House paintings. Just after we bought the house, we acquired her painting *State Dining Room,* which now hangs in the living room. It's so perfect because we love this artist, the picture is of the State Dining Room, and it's hanging in the living room of the former president's home."

In their thoughtful renovation of the Ford estate, McIlwee and Damaschke have created a house that pays homage to the past while being a celebration of their own interests, tastes, and desires. "We're passionate about responsibility, preservation, and the way we live," says McIlwee. "We cannot continue to live the way we have been, our earth cannot sustain it. My ambition is to further the conversation about substantial architecture and design. It's our responsibility in order to keep living in a world that's creative and interesting and collaborative."

CAMDEN

THOMAS PENN
WINTER KING
JEAN GENET
Querelle of Brest
Retro Fonts
Graphic Design for the 21st Century
THE SUN KING
DAN BROWN
ORLANDO
Nigel Slater
THE GLASGOW COOKERY BOOK
THE RIVER CAFE COOK BOOK
EPICUREAN
COCKTAIL
EDWARD ST AUBYN
THE PHOTO BOOK
THE ART BOOK
Polaroids
THE STRANGER'S CHILD
ALAN HOLLINGHURST
WILLIAM BOYD ANY HUMAN HEART
JOHNNY SCOTT
A BOOK OF BRITAIN
THE GUGGENHEIM
LONDON
TRACEY EMIN
DELUXE
THE BOOK of MAGIC
FOLLY GRANDEUR
ANTIQUES

DUNCAN CAMPBELL & LUKE EDWARD HALL

Duncan Campbell bought his Camden flat aged just nineteen. "It was quite grown up," he says, with understatement. "At the time I was the editor of *Acne Paper* and studying law at King's College. The place was completely trashed, needed a complete gut out, to be rewired, replumbed, all that boring stuff. Luke moved in a couple of years later, and now we decorate it recreationally."

Today Duncan is cofounder of creative and design consultancy Campbell-Rey. Luke is artist and designer Luke Edward Hall, Campbell's boyfriend of nearly a decade, and collaborator in decorative recreation. Together they have authored a brand of joyful, adventurous maximalism that blends color, clashing prints, literary inspiration, painted furniture, Positano ceramics, and Greco-Roman figures to the delight of fashion brands, interiors magazines, and an ever-growing audience of Instagram followers.

Their Camden flat has become an incubator of ideas, taking on the various roles of home, studio, and showroom. "Your taste evolves, of course," says Campbell. "Really you just get better furniture. But we don't swing between different styles—it's never going to be arts and crafts one minute, then all white like a John Porter house the next."

Life&Arts
Beatniks — a gift to capitalism
Janan Ganesh
Citizen of nowhere
Can a sweater help us talk about abortion?
PHOTO LONDON
MADNESS
GOLDFINCH
DONNA TARTT
House&Home
Do Not Buy This House

Stem
subjects

"I think that's why we're a good pair," says Hall, "because I would always go mega Bloomsbury Group in my style, not traditional but painted things, painted furniture, and Duncan would always go more mid-century. So it works well." The eclecticism of the couple's home makes a nonsense of the notion that smaller spaces should be kept neutral in color and minimal in design. An egg-yolk yellow hallway spills into a pink drawing room; the bedroom's malachite-printed wallpaper is offset with pink velvet curtains and a leopard-print carpet; art deco mirrors and Jean Cocteau prints cover the walls, while the surfaces offer a jumble of Hall's own ceramics, Ettore Sottsass sculptures,

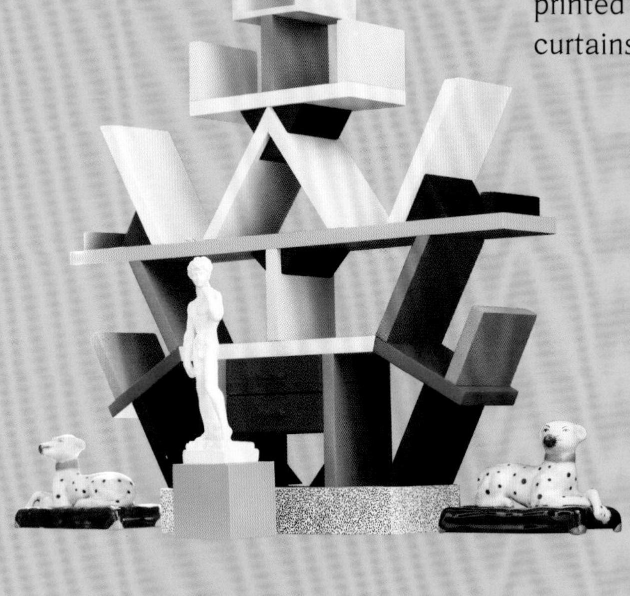

and Staffordshire figurines. The house is forever a work in progress. With the bedroom recently updated, they now have the kitchen in their sights. "We're thinking cobalt blue, shiny, lacquered," says Hall. "With fun, hand-painted Amalfi tiles in the back," adds Campbell. They are unsentimental about switching it up. "We don't get too attached to stuff. You love something for a while, then you get bored of it and you pass it on to someone else," Campbell says. Hall agrees. "The things that mean the most are the little things. The Michelangelo statue I bought from a tourist shop in Rome,

on my first trip to Italy when I was seventeen, the little ashtray we bought from Amalfi. Obviously I love the sofa and the coffee table, but our treasures are the things that have a story." The lines between work and home are necessarily blurred when a personal aesthetic is part of the business, and using Instagram as a showcase for their work, and their flat as their showroom, can be hazardous. "We post pictures of stuff, and people immediately write and ask to buy them," Campbell explains. "I'm much less attached to things I've made. Once I've done it, I'm done with it." For Hall it's more emotional. "Because they are hand-painted ceramics, they are quite special. I want to be able to look back in ten years and think, I remember making that. If I sell everything, I won't." For a couple so motivated by travel and new horizons, it is perhaps surprising they have remained for so long in this uncelebrated corner of North London. "It's a weird bit of town here," Campbell admits. "It's not Camden proper, kind of tucked away, full of dotty old professor types, and it's ten years behind everywhere else—we only just got our first hipster coffee shop. But it's all listed and can't be changed, so you won't suddenly get a tower at the end of the road." While they don't foresee leaving London for good, they have rented a cottage in the Gloucestershire countryside for weekends, creating yet another interiors wonderland for Instagram to swoon over. Here Hall got his "chintz sofas and acid green walls," while Campbell has offset the dollhouse effect with mid-century design and twentieth-century furniture. And if they had to leave the UK? "Venice would be the dream," says Hall. "We could rent a piano nobile on the Grand Canal for a few months," muses Campbell. "There is something in the air in Venice, creativity and magic. But it's also a nightmarish place to run a business. Imagine the FedEx man having to hire a boat . . ."

Dorothy Cross:
Connemara
5 October 2013
– 5 January 2014
turnercontemporary.org
HOTEL
CIPRIANI

STP
STP
SRM 15X

ROSA DE LA CRUZ

Entering Rosa de la Cruz's Chelsea home is like walking into the best contemporary art gallery you didn't know existed. Every surface in her two huge, light-filled reception rooms, all the way through to the more private spaces at the back of the house, is filled with extraordinary pieces that tell the story not only of de la Cruz's decades-long passion for art, but also the shifting movements and preoccupations that have taken hold of the art world over that time.

"I started collecting in my early twenties," she says. "At the time painting was out of fashion, and everyone wanted installations, video art, photography. One of the earliest works in my collection is a painting by the Brazilian artist Beatriz Milhazes, but it isn't really painting in the traditional sense. When we moved to London in the late nineties, it was all about the YBA movement and I started collecting works by Tracey Emin, Gary Hume, Chris Ofili, and Damien Hirst, and an early Peter Doig. Later in the collection you see works that typify what could be loosely known as process art—again, paintings that defy traditional technique—by American artists Christopher Wool, Wade Guyton, Nate Lowman, and now, in works by artist Glenn Ligon, there's a focus on confronting issues of gender, race, and sexuality."

The recent addition of a vast painting by Laura Owens not only illustrates how de la Cruz's collection is constantly evolving to reflect shifting preoccupations, but also the issues that occasionally face the dedicated collector. "It is so large, we had to cut out the window and door frame to get it into the flat," de la Cruz laughs.

The design pieces are as jaw-dropping as the art, featuring works by Jean Royère, Charlotte Perriand, Mathieu Matégot, and Jean Prouvé. Every object is significant—ashtrays are by Sterling Ruby, a ceramic dish is by Georges Jouve, and de la Cruz's extensive collection of Ettore Sottsass totems can be found dotted throughout the house. "I take joy in beautiful things," she says.

As the daughter of Carlos and Rosa de la Cruz, renowned collectors and founders of the de la Cruz Contemporary Art Space in Miami's Design

District, de la Cruz's passion for art runs in the family. Her first career, however, was as an attorney at the Guggenheim Museum in New York, and she now designs an eponymous jewelry line with former *Harper's Bazaar* fashion director Tierney Horne. "I'm constantly juggling my million interests," she says. "I need a longer day for all my activities."

These activities include being mother to four boys aged from fifteen to twenty-three. Her sons may officially be away—the elder two at Georgetown University, the younger two at boarding school—but they are often at home, a fact rendered unsurprising on discovering that their bedrooms are filled with bright furniture by Marni and lined with Damien Hirst's series *The Last Supper*.

There is a deliberate shift in tone between the momentous front living rooms and the more private spaces at the rear of the flat, which include the family's bedrooms—a move from large dramatic canvases to more intimate works on paper. A little bathroom has early Tracey Emin drawings while de la Cruz's bedroom is filled with her extensive collection of Chris Ofili's watercolor portraits.

The corridor's black walls—a decorating feat achieved by de la Cruz's boyfriend, Marc Reynier, with her assistance—create a dramatic backdrop for a series by Mark Bradford, although there are down-sides. "Black is the highest-maintenance color possible," she says ruefully. "If you even touch the walls, you see the marks, so my boys know they have to be super careful."

De la Cruz has lived on Cadogan Square for twenty-two years and in her current house for a decade. She knew it was right the minute she walked in—"I'm an Island girl, I need light"—despite its dire need of renovation.

"The flat belonged to an English music composer and his family, and it had not been touched since the eighties. There were gold initials on the bathroom sinks, gold swan taps, I lost sleep over the gilded fireplace." A radical revamp saw the creation of a front hall—"a buffer zone"—and the kitchen enclosed into an airy box, while a mezzanine and library were taken out to return the two ballrooms to their original lofty scale, ready to house de la Cruz's ever-expanding collection.

"I am a collector at heart, but I'm a minimalist," she says. "I'm constantly cleaning up and constantly editing. I have so many things I love, it's amazing to be able to surround myself with them, move them around, get something new from them every day."

SALT FAT ACID HEAT Samin Nosrat
Jim Lahey MY PIZZA
REDZEPI
WHAT KATIE ATE
NG I WANT TO EAT Koslow
ENTINE Emiko Davies

Richard Christiansen

A few years ago, a friend asked Richard Christiansen if he would help his elderly neighbor John install a beehive in his garden in Eagle Rock, Northeast LA. Christiansen is best known as the founder and creative director of Chandelier Creative, but as the son of Australian horticulturalists and an avid beekeeper, he was happy to oblige.

He crossed the road to be met by an old man in a red silk bathrobe, living alone in a pink 1940s house set in a vast, unruly garden. "It was like Grey Gardens, just falling apart," Christiansen remembers. "I was never allowed inside, but I took a photo of the place on Google Maps and made it my screen saver for a year. I thought, 'One day I'm going to own that house.'" Fast-forward to 2013, and there came the phone call—would he like to buy it? "I thought, 'This is crazy,' and signed a check."

When Christiansen finally crossed the threshold, he found seven decades of Los Angeles history piled high. John and his partner, Ralph, had lived there for sixty-five years, running an erotic film studio, a pirate radio station, a fanzine publishing company, a political fundraising team as well as a retreat for countercultural photographers and artists, and never throwing anything away.

"They created an enclave where there was a lot of sex, a lot of art, a lot of music, and a lot of parties," says Christiansen. "It was a haven for extroverts, a safe place to go wild." The house may have changed hands and shape, but Christiansen has stayed true to its disposition. "I believe deeply in the idea of genius loci, the protective spirit of a place. This house's spirit came from an amazing tapestry of people who were a bit naughty, a bit crazy, a bit wonderful. I arrived to take it into the next era."

The Flamingo Estate—named by Christiansen for its pink walls and proud stance—marked a new era for him too. After more than fifteen years in Manhattan, founding advertising agency Chandelier Creative and leading its game-changing work with brands including Old Navy, Cartier, Lane Crawford, and Virgin, as well as directing a stadium tour for Kylie Minogue, Christiansen arrived on the West Coast exhausted. "I was so burnt out, I was sick of advertising.

Le Corbusier
DONALD
Beautiful People
The Landscape Designs of Doyle Herman Design Associates
WORLD'S BEST TYPE
SAN FRANCISCO NOIR
Merce Cunningham
CO:MM:ON TI:ME
DREAMLANDS: IMMERSIVE CINEMA AND ART, 1905–2016
ROBERT ADAM
FRANÇOIS HALARD
Dior THE ART of COLOR
nurture
STATION

Peter
Lindbergh

I wanted to be inspired again, and LA is the birthplace of the world's imagination. It was a fresh start."

He enlisted the help of Paris-based architects Karl Fournier and Olivier Marty of Studio KO, whom he met while they were consulting on André Balazs's Chiltern Firehouse. "I was interested to work with them because I had never been on the other side of the table. They taught me so much, particularly in the way they grounded their thoughts in storytelling. I went to Morocco, India, Asia

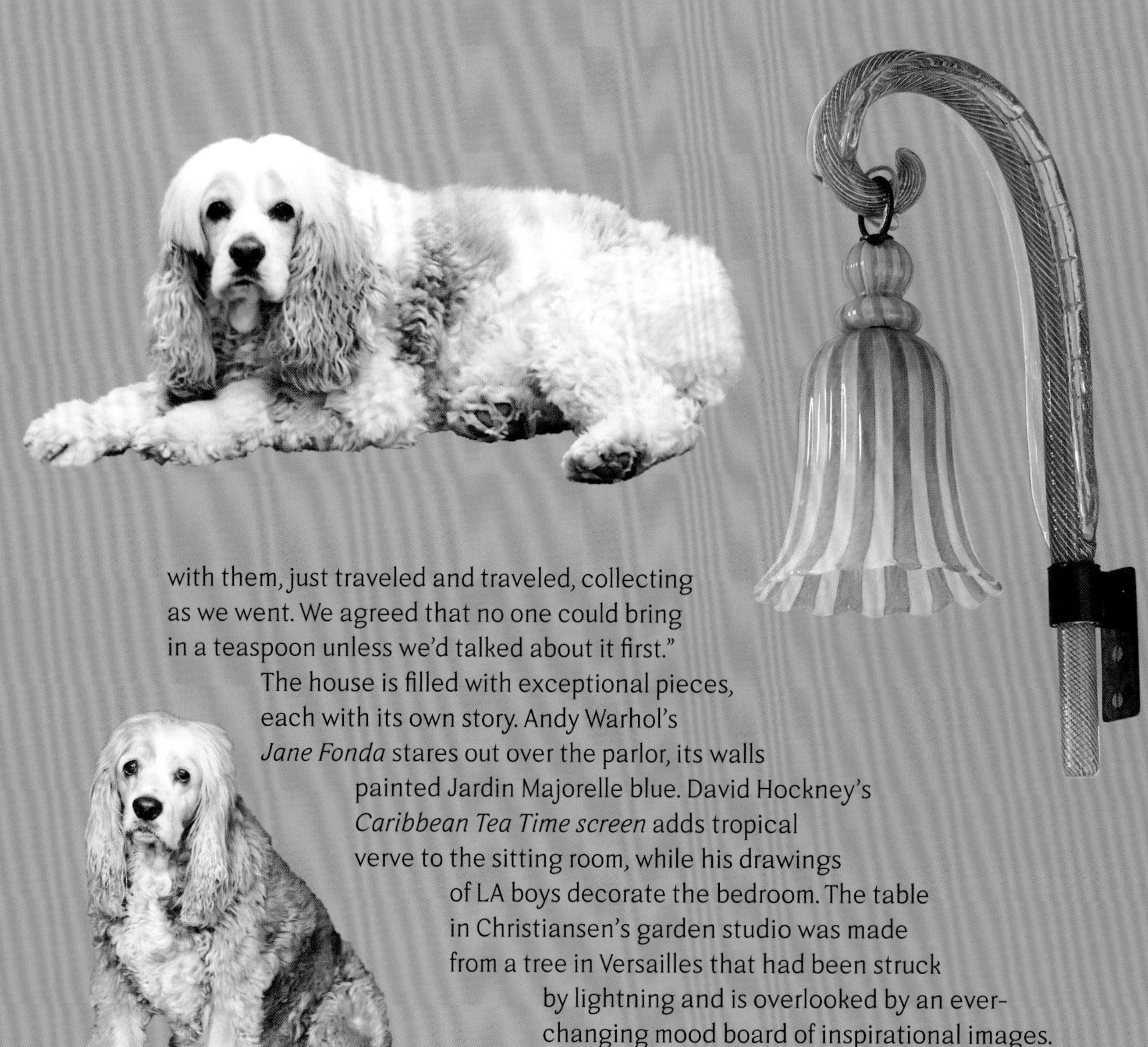

with them, just traveled and traveled, collecting as we went. We agreed that no one could bring in a teaspoon unless we'd talked about it first."

The house is filled with exceptional pieces, each with its own story. Andy Warhol's *Jane Fonda* stares out over the parlor, its walls painted Jardin Majorelle blue. David Hockney's *Caribbean Tea Time screen* adds tropical verve to the sitting room, while his drawings of LA boys decorate the bedroom. The table in Christiansen's garden studio was made from a tree in Versailles that had been struck by lightning and is overlooked by an ever-changing mood board of inspirational images.

FEARLESS
·LIVING·JEAN-

He spends his days between here and the poured concrete bathtub, which is housed in a staggering 400-square-foot, three-story monolith inspired by ruins in the Atlas Mountains. "I call it the Bathing Cathedral, and it is my place of worship. It was the first room I built. I'm there for two hours every day and night." His other obsession is the 7-acre garden,

created in collaboration with landscape designer Arnaud Casaus. A lush Eden full of fruit, vegetables, chickens, bees, and tobacco (which is dried for estate-grown cigarettes), it hides a red-glazed pool deck overlooked by two vast palmyra palms found for $30 on Craigslist. Nearly a thousand trees were newly planted across the estate, as well as flowers, cacti, herb bushes, and palms, which now play host to butterflies, owls, and hummingbirds. Getting back to nature was what motivated Christiansen's move from east to west, and the green economy is now the focus of his formidable vision. "As a community, we are feeling a collective anxiety that is sending us running back to nature, but there is no one there to catch us. My plan is to disrupt the gardening sector, to produce beautiful, well-made

products for the garden with all the proceeds going towards climate change." Christiansen's hero is Walt Disney, and the Flamingo Estate, in all its Moroccan-tiled, pink-bricked glory, is his Epcot Center. As he grew up on a huge farm in Australia "my parents couldn't make money from farming, so they bused in tourists for the 'Outback experience.' My brother and I came home from school and threw frozen crabs in the crab pots to make them believe they had caught a real one. We tied Cabbage Patch dolls to the backs of sheep so the tourists could have races. At night we watched *Dynasty* and dreamed of America, Joan Collins, and her Louis Vuitton luggage. My childhood was about the exercise of make-believe from necessity. My work is about conjuring dreams for clients. With this house I've made my dreams come true."

AIR FRANCE

Louise Bourgeois
George Ohr

GRAHAM STEELE & ULYSSES DE SANTI

Walking into the West Hollywood home of gallerist Graham Steele and furniture dealer Ulysses de Santi, it is immediately clear the couple love their work.

The town house is furnished with Brazilian modernist masterpieces sourced by de Santi and hung with a staggering collection of work by contemporary artists whom Steele has either worked with or long admired.

"These are our highlights," says de Santi. For Steele, just looking round the sitting room is to take a roll call of friends and fond memories—an Anne Truitt painting he bought with de Santi in mind, wedding presents from Christian Marclay and Raqib Shaw, a piece by Luchita Hurtado, a vast Anselm Kiefer, a sculpture by Mona Hatoum.

But finding the perfect setting for this exceptional assemblage was not straightforward. The couple moved to Los Angeles in 2015, as Steele took up a new role at Hauser & Wirth. "Neither of us had ever lived here, so we didn't want to buy straightaway," explains de Santi. Instead they set up in a rental in Boystown, West Hollywood, and started searching. "I literally looked at every house on the market. I went to open houses every Tuesday and Sunday for two years. This was the first house we both fell in love with immediately."

"It was the one," agrees Steele. "The house was warm, the proportions were generous, and with nothing but white walls, it was basically a gallery.

But Ulysses has the worst poker face ever, so I had to glare at him to stop him from getting overexcited in front of the realtor." "The whole idea of Californian open living, it was never something that fascinated me," explains de Santi. "I love rooms, and this house has rooms, so that made me very happy." Finding the right house at that moment was a stroke of good luck. "We had just got married and were deeply depressed," says Steele. "We'd had

the most beautiful wedding in Rio, and we came back to LA in January, looked at each other, and said, 'We need a project.'" The house required some restructuring, including the removal of interior walls to open up the ground floor and the addition of a wall of glass doors in the living room to let in maximum sunlight. The walls stayed white, of course, while de Santi stained the floors a matte black to offset the wood of the Brazilian furniture. "There is the delineation that I focus on the art and Ulysses on the furniture, but we do move back and forth," explains Steele. "But Ulysses sometimes has strong feelings about the art, and he usually wins out." Against the monochrome backdrop, works by Luiz Zerbini, Carroll Dunham, Nicola Martini, Frank Bowling, and Pae White are arresting counterpoints to Joaquim Tenreiro's bench, a red velvet Neobox sofa, Jorge Zalszupin cube chairs, glass vases by Jacqueline Terpins, and a rare prototype of an Oscar Niemeyer chaise, which sits in the master bedroom and is de Santi's

We Love you
SINGER
SINGER

pick for his favorite piece in the house. "It's so rare, so iconic, and so amazing to wake up to every morning."

Asking Steele to pick a favorite prompts a wince: "It's so hard, but I love this Larry Bell cube that I bought early on when I was starting to intervene in his career. Now when I look at it, I see our relationship and what I've been able to do with him, how meeting him shaped my career, and how a deep passion for an artist can really make a difference."

Bell is integral to the couple as it was his 2014 solo show in São Paulo that took Steele to Brazil and led to his meeting with de Santi. "We are weird freaks of nature," says Steele. "Ulysses moved in the first time we ever met each other, and we immediately had this relationship as if we had been together forever."

This is not to say the couple does not have their differences. "If it were up to me," says Steele, "everything in this house would be covered in objects. I've traveled all over the world, and I love collecting aide-mémoire, things that tell the story of my life and where I've been."

"Which is my worst nightmare," groans de Santi. "He is such a maximalist; he wants all these things out on display. But I think of the furniture as artworks, and the idea of hiding them under a million objects is a tragedy. So every time he brings something back and puts it out, I wait for him to travel again and I put it in a closet."

"It's like a scavenger hunt in reverse," Steele laughs ruefully. But this is a rare moment of disagreement for the pair, whose shared ethos extends beyond furniture and art into how they use and enjoy their home—throwing it open to friends visiting from overseas as well as hosting frequent dinner parties. Lucky guests are advised to make a visit to the downstairs powder room, which deviates from the white-wall rule with raucous Damien Hirst wallpaper and artwork: gifts from the artist, of course.

For Steele and de Santi, the possibility of art or design fatigue is dismissed without question. "We don't even think of this as work," says de Santi. "I'm just so happy to live with these pieces that I'm so passionate about, and I love the idea that I get to go and find more of them. That's my job? It's 100 percent pleasure."

PROJECTIONS 8
FOREVER BUTT
Still Moving
GENESIS
ART STUDIO AMERICA
gutai
BEEFCAKE
FEMINIST ART

MARIE-LOUISE SCIÒ

Marie-Louise Sciò can take credit for a lot at Il Pellicano. As creative director of the famed hotel at Porto Ercole, on Italy's Tuscan coast, she is responsible for designing the now iconic yellow-and-white-striped towels, for streamlining the bathrooms, and for helping reignite the magical atmosphere captured by Slim Aarons in his 1970s photographs. But the oldest item on her CV dates back to her childhood.

"The no children rule is the result of my misbehavior here as a kid," she confesses. "It was always like a grown-ups' living room and I wasn't allowed downstairs, so I was always going round the back of the bedrooms and breaking in. The first time I saw anyone have sex was here—my brother and I spied through a keyhole!"

Sciò's father, Roberto, bought Il Pellicano in 1979, so she grew up scrambling up and down the tiers between its shady bungalows and cliff-edge sun loungers. After training as an architect and a stint in New York designing furniture, Sciò returned to Rome in 2005. "I decided I needed an Italian boyfriend and a good football team," she says. "My father had other ideas—he asked if I could redo bathrooms."

Having made a success of the bathroom project, Sciò advised her father to give Il Pellicano a face-lift. "It was going well but it had had its glory days, and I could see it fading. He said, 'Do it!' I turned him down, because I was too young, too inexperienced, but then I interviewed other architects and no one got the spirit of the place. I thought, well, I'll probably fuck it up but I'll fuck it up less. So I redid all of the main building. By myself, over three years."

Sciò's refresh of the hotel was inspired by its history as one of the world's iconic hotels, her design evoking a style that is modern, beautiful, fresh, but also somehow a time warp, a tribute to the spirit of its first heyday that Aarons recorded for posterity.

"That's what I wanted to capitalize on," she says. "The energy of the past as well as the future. I wanted to give the place an update but keep the original parts, keep the layers of life that have built up over the years,

PORTO

the elements that keep drawing people back." She even got her own celebrated photographer to commemorate the reboot, recruiting Juergen Teller to take a series of seminal shots in 2010. The best hotels have an atmosphere that is hard to define, a sense of being at home while being treated like kings, of everything being informal yet extraordinary at the same time. "It's like a recipe—you need good elements," Sciò says. "Will Self used a great Italian word to describe this place: 'sprezzatura'—the concealed art of effortless good taste. There is a magic in this place; it's totally its own time zone. No one comes here to prove anything—people drop their jewelry and their egos at the door."

Today Sciò is creative director for the whole Pellicano group, her flair for design and hospitality visible at La Posta Vecchia, J. Paul Getty's villa near Rome, and Mezzatorre on the island of Ischia.

For some, renovating and updating such beloved, historic places would be an intimidating commission, but Sciò is only excited by the challenge. "Being confident in knowing the places and feeling their spirit means there is no anxiety or need to leave my stamp on the place. I can be subtle. It's already there."

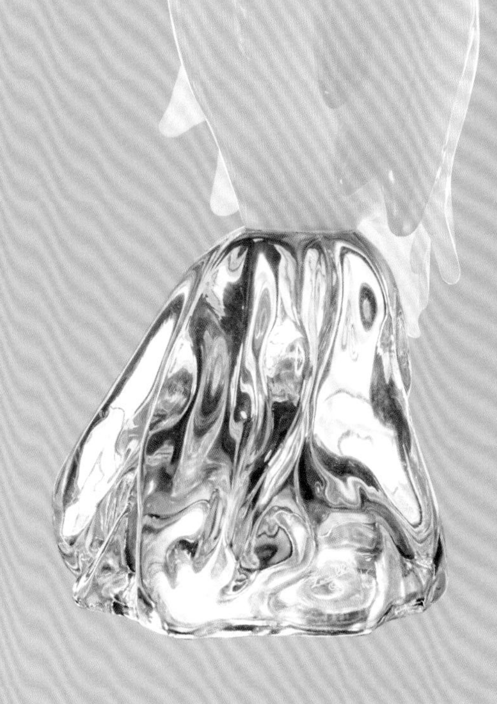

From their seafront bungalow overlooking Sydney's Tamarama Bay, Tamsin and Patrick Johnson would appear to be living the definitive Australian dream. With Tamsin gaining renown as one of the country's foremost interior designers and Patrick providing a distinctly antipodean take on both men's and women's tailoring with his brand P. Johnson, the couple have become ambassadors for the Australian lifestyle.

"Australia's incredible," Tamsin says simply. "We're beach people and the summer is very long, our families are nearby, it's a calmer way of life."

But part of the Johnsons' appreciation of their homeland comes from the time they are away from it. Tamsin became intimately familiar with Europe growing up, spending her school holidays tagging along on her antique dealer parents' collecting trips to France, Italy, and Spain. Patrick spent formative years in Europe, studying wine in France before moving to London to do menswear at Central Saint Martins.

"Travel helps you think about the bigger picture," Tamsin says. "In order to see things and get inspired, you do need to travel the world. Even though we're so far away in Australia, we don't really feel the distance. Europe, America, Asia—we have an open mind to going everywhere."

After a stint living in New York, the couple moved to Sydney in 2017 on discovering Tamsin was pregnant with their first child. Neither had lived in the city before, and they were attracted by the call of the new. "I like the challenge of a new place," says Tamsin. "Meeting people, exploring, and going down streets for the first time rather than replicating the life that your parents have done just for the sake of it." Vitally, the move meant finding a new home. A chance online sighting of a 1960s bungalow in a tiny coastal suburb saw the couple viewing, bidding on, and acquiring their new house within twenty-

four hours. "The same lady had been living there for fifty years; it hadn't been touched since it was built," remembers Tamsin. "So we gutted the whole thing, opened up all the walls to create a big beautiful open-plan space. I don't always love open plan, but this place just needed to celebrate the view and bring the outside in and be an extension of that." Embracing the color and light that pour in through the wall of seafront-facing windows, Tamsin has created an interior that nods to the freshness of the coastal Australian climate, the reality of family living—they now have two children, Arthur and Bunny—and the passion for collecting that she and Patrick share. "It encapsulates my style because it expresses what I strive

TAMARAMA S.L.S.C.

GJELINA
PLACES WE SWIM

for in all my interiors," she says. "It's comfortable, not too formal. It's a calm and neutral backdrop, a lot more texture than color, formed of important, interesting pieces from different periods that work together."

This ease and neutrality are essential as the house also operates as an incubator, somewhere Tamsin can try pieces out before they move onto her showroom floor or are sent out to clients. "It's a gallery space," she says. "I like challenging it with different things to see what works. It keeps me realistic, and it keeps me ambitious as to what's possible."

She credits her upbringing for her unsentimental attitude to furniture —"my norm as a child was having different pieces of furniture come and go before my eyes the whole time, so that definitely had an impact on my awareness of different elements of design and furniture, as well as taking pleasure in things changing."

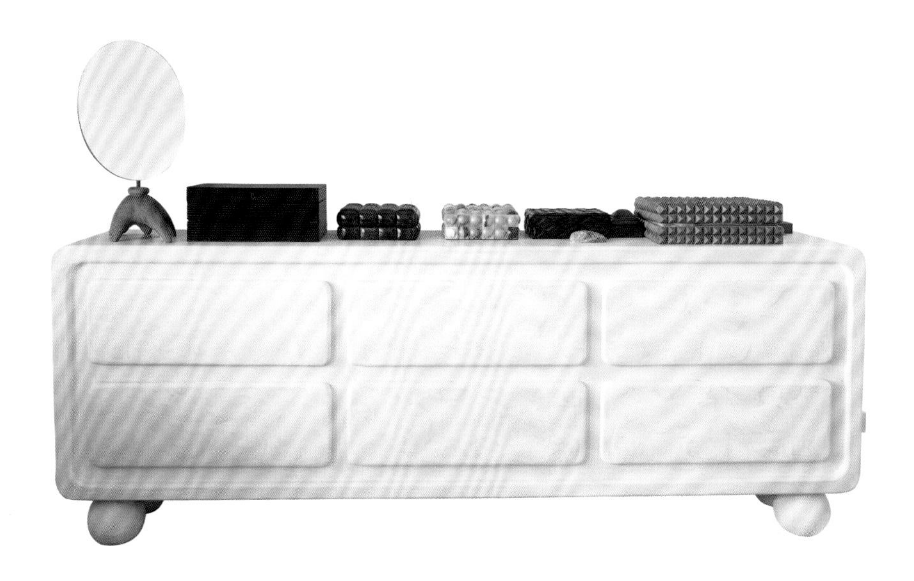

While the coffee table may be at risk—"we've had four since moving in" —the Johnsons' art collection is not for sale. With a lineup that is long on contemporary Australian artists including painters Kirsty Budge and Luke Sciberras, photographer Trent Parke, and sculptor Brendan Huntley, the collection speaks to the Johnsons' interest in their community, while a wealth of 1930s abstract art from Europe, photography, an Alexander Calder-style mobile on the pool deck, and a vivid work by the Italian postwar artist Pino Manos demonstrate a curious eye.

"I love the balance of not just collecting one thing," Tamsin says. "Things look good when pieces have been brought together through the common language of someone truly loving everything. If someone trusts their own taste, has that confidence, it will all work together."

SIBYLLE ROCHAT

For the art consultant Sibylle Rochat, decorating a house is no simple matter.

"I like to live in a picture," she says. "I have a picture in my head and my house has to fit that image, otherwise I feel very unsettled."

Unsurprisingly, it is her art collection that makes the picture, playing the central role in her West London home. Her interiors are sharp and pared back, dotted with work Rochat has acquired over twenty years working as an art consultant, first at Christie's in New York, then in Geneva for Marc Blondeau, before striking out under her own name in Paris and London.

"I am not a knickknack person," she says. "I don't have photographs in frames or random objects. I admire the freedom of other people who do, but I keep it strict. That's my way of functioning and recharging my battery in my house."

This discipline means that everything in Rochat's house is a talking point. A striped piece in the hallway is a Daniel Buren corridorscope from the eighties, while Robert Rauschenberg's *Jungle Jam* has pride of place in the dining room, facing off with a work by the young Brooklyn artist Landon Metz. A John Baldessari represents Rochat's admiration for an artist "who managed to build a bridge between pop art and conceptual art," while a sculpture of a stubbed-out cigarette simply "made me laugh."

Separating the kitchen and dining room is a concrete screen by Mark Hagen—"it's the only piece of art I have bought that has been actually useful," Rochat laughs. Yet still it caused a headache. "Hanging a house for me is complicated. I have moved this piece four times, each time about 8 inches, but it's still not quite right. But every time I want to move it, I need to get two movers to dismantle it, and a specialist to check all the pieces are correctly positioned. It's one of the downsides to furnishing your house with art."

The upside is the story that it tells. "My art collection is really personal," she says. "What lives with me is really what I like." A particularly emotive piece is a work by Mohamed Bourouissa, a film still of a boy, tinged blue, mounted on a piece of scrap metal.

THE GRAND
BAZAAR
ISTANBUL
ASSOULINE

"I think this is both the cornerstone and also the crossroads of my taste," Rochat explains. "I love video art, I love music. It's very sculptural, it's got that rough aesthetic, the feel of an abandoned yard." She goes on, "I like a very nice interior, everything has to be aligned, but then in art I like different, wilder stuff. More disordered." Contrasting styles denote different areas in the house. A lively series of human-sized John Miller cutouts travels up the stairs, while in the bedroom the energy is more intimate, with a framed nude by Zoran Mušič, a delicate sculpture by Evan Holloway,

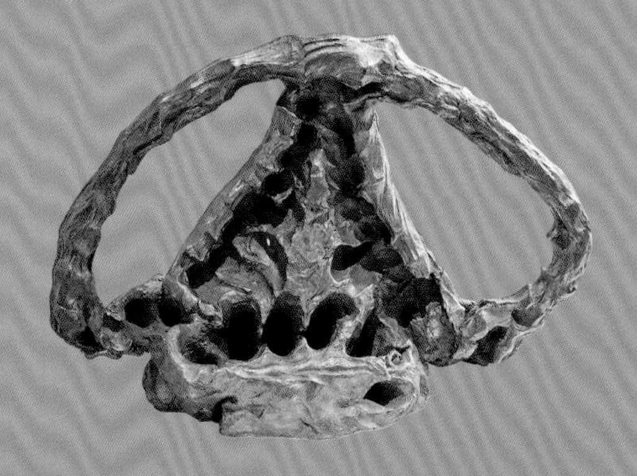

and a drawing by her daughter Camilla propped up on the chest of drawers. She alighted on this area of West London in part because of its inimitable Englishness. "I like the Chelsea vibe, a lot of old British people around me, it's like a little corner of the countryside." A huge work by Gilbert & George in the living room is a nod to her adopted home. "The UK is an island with very specific taste. When I arrived I had very Swiss taste, very minimalist, and in London everyone has an Anish Kapoor, everyone has a Damien Hirst. I bought my Gilbert & George for its flavor of London." London's siren call was its energy. "I came here for work, to be somewhere more dynamic. You can lose yourself, you can have five different lives in five different areas. I love that anonymity, the eccentricity, the freedom. I feel like I have access to everything. Brexit makes it difficult, the rules are changing every day, but it's home now and I hope I can stay here forever."

Rebecca Warren
Rebecca Warren
FUEL
Giotto
Tiepolo
de Chirico
Go Figure! New Perspectives on Guston
Perspectives on Guston
AMERICAN ACADEMY IN ROME
NEW YORK REVIEW BOOKS

It comes as no surprise that Sarah Harris's house in Notting Hill, London, is an exercise in pared-back refinement.

As deputy editor of British *Vogue,* Harris is a mainstay of best-dressed lists, easily picked out in the fashion crowd by her long silver hair and tailored elegance. Her home is similarly singular, designed and built from the ground up by Harris and her husband, Alfie Hollingsworth.

"We were living in a garden flat near Ladbroke Grove, and then the small house next door came up for sale. My husband had always liked the spot on the street, so we bought it with a view to knocking down the existing house and building something entirely different."

The couple stayed in their flat for the duration of the build—a mixed blessing. "On the one hand it was great as it meant we could stay on top of the project. On the other hand it was the worst, because we just couldn't escape it. I found it quite stressful trying to picture what I wanted. I can't get a feel for a place as a floor plan. I need walls to help me visualize."

But despite her initial anxieties, Harris's vision for the house worked, and nearly a decade on, the couple have made no alterations—with one significant exception. "We have a daughter, Dree, who has obviously changed everything. Not least our living room, which is now overrun by a huge dollhouse."

New furniture was very much on Harris's mind when the house was finished. "I moved in with my husband when we got together, and it was very much his place and his furniture. So it was exciting to have an excuse to go out and buy some nice things that I wanted around me, to live with, rather than just his things that were quite bachelor. We didn't buy everything all at once. We lived in the space for a bit, and picked up pieces over time, like the lights that we found in a Brussels antiques shop and the Caroline Popham artwork that came from Alex Eagle Studio."

A lithograph by Pablo Picasso featuring a typically disjointed female face with a long ponytail has become a family joke. "I liked it because of the long hair, but whenever my daughter and I head upstairs for a bath, she points at it and says, 'Mama.' She recognizes my hair in it, but I don't know what it says about how she sees my face." The house extends over three floors, with Harris's favorite being the one at the top.

"I love spending time up there, it's a real sanctuary. It's our bedroom and

bathroom, with the walk-in wardrobe connecting the two." Of course, the wardrobe was a big deal. "I'd never had a big enough wardrobe before, and so I worked with a carpenter to create the perfect design, with glass drawers. I wanted it to feel luxurious, like a jewelry box, which inspired the leather cladding on the walls. I spent weeks puzzling over what color to have until I found the teal, which works so well with the pink walls and green curtains."

The color was not the only wardrobe conundrum Harris faced. "My husband and I argued over the real estate of that wardrobe for ages, battling over percentages of space. I wanted it all to be mine, but eventually we compromised on a 70/30 percent split. But every few months I steal another drawer." Notting Hill has now been Harris's home for over fifteen years. "I can't imagine living anywhere else, I think it's the nicest place to be in London." As for the house, "it works for us for now, but I'm not so attached to it that I could never see us leaving it. It's such a nice thing to have done and to have built and to know—hope—that it will be here longer than we will."

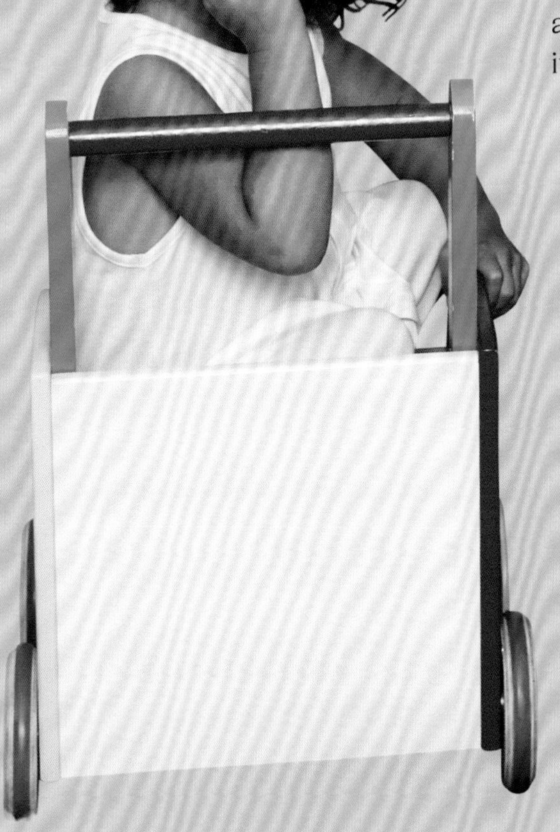

diptyque 34 boulevard saint germain
FIGUIER
paris 5e

ROBERTO RUSPOLI

For the artist Roberto Ruspoli, his hometown consists of a single street. “Rome is Via Margutta,” he says. “This is my area. I don’t go anywhere I can’t walk to from here.”

It is easy to see why. From his rooftop studio above Margutta’s wisteria-lined cobblestones, Ruspoli has sweeping views across the city. “I am a bit claustrophobic, so I like air. This house feels like a ship traveling through the sky. At night you can see the moon through the windows. It’s magic.”

There is magic closer to the ground too. Born in Lugano, an Italian-speaking city in Switzerland, Ruspoli moved to the house with his mother and stepfather as a child. “Via Margutta has always been traditionally for artists,” he says. “Pablo Picasso worked here, and Federico Fellini lived on this street. I grew up seeing Fellini riding his bicycle up and down. All these interesting people living here, it was inspiring.”

Perhaps it was this environment that prompted Ruspoli’s mother to try and distract her crying son with art. “She discovered that the moment she gave me a piece of paper and a pen, I would go silent and start to draw,” he remembers.

Art remains a calming experience. “I have explored different languages, but in the end I went back to what I did as a kid. In painting, the color is the body, but the drawing is the soul, the structure of it all. What interests me is what happens inside me when I’m drawing. It’s like walking a tightrope: you have to concentrate very hard, find a state of mind that is meditative, become an instrument of a flow.”

Evidence of Ruspoli’s work is everywhere in his apartment. His classical and Jean Cocteau–infused figures comport themselves on every surface, drawn directly onto the walls in charcoal. “It’s my little factory,” he says, “I consider it more an atelier than a normal apartment, it’s where I come to draw and create, and it changes all the time.”

The house itself is minimalist, all white except its terracotta tiled floor. “I painted the roof white myself. I wanted a blank canvas, a white page.

Edgar Degas
POTSDAM
DOSSO DOSSI

It's nice because it leaves my head clear to
imagine new things, to be neutral."
The few pieces of furniture date from its time
as Ruspoli's family home. "I'm not attached
very much to objects in general," he says.
"I like places where the objects in the house are
part of its history, to have layers of things
in time that add up and create a narrative."
His books are his most prized possessions—

"they are my life story"—as well as a photograph
taken by a friend of a performance by Pina
Bausch's Tanztheater Wuppertal.
"I took part in a Pina Bausch show, *O Dido*,
and it was one of the most extraordinary
experiences of my life. It helped me in my art,
to become unblocked. Rarely in our lives do
we come into contact with such a powerful
source of creativity." A lineup of statues and
objects overlooking the sitting room speaks
to the eighteen months Ruspoli spent in
Lecce teaching himself ceramics. "It is a very

BALTHUS

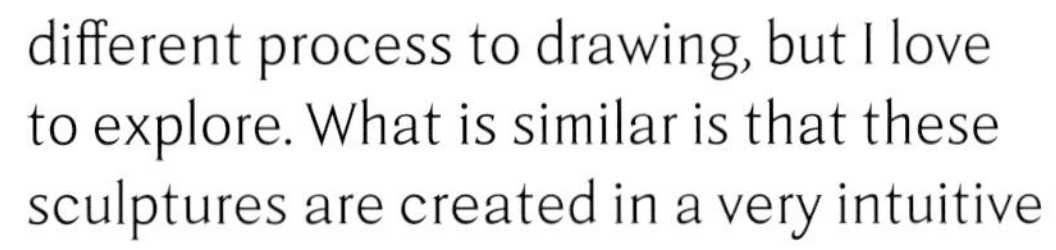

different process to drawing, but I love to explore. What is similar is that these sculptures are created in a very intuitive way, through feeling and touching." The latest additions are two light fittings, two of Ruspoli's male profiles carved by Milan artisans Servomuto. "They do haute couture for lamps and this is really exciting, to see one of my designs

transformed into a three-dimensional object." At the moment Ruspoli splits his time between Rome and Paris, where home is an atelier that once belonged to Fernand Léger. "It has a real atmosphere, but it is where I live and work so it's a big mess. I come back to Rome for some detachment. Here is where I think, I get inspired, I make drawings and studies, and I don't mess up. Paris is the working place." Sitting on the roof terrace, with its unmatched views across to Villa Medici, Ruspoli considers his surroundings. "Let's be honest, Rome is the most beautiful city in the world in terms of architecture, but as an artist it's hard to feel free when you are confronted by the weight of its heritage. In Paris there is a lightness that I can't find here."

Indrė Šerpytytė

A Scottish castle comes with expectations for its interiors—dark wood, heavy upholstery, suits of armor perhaps, chilly hallways of course, and most likely a ghost or two.

Fine-art photographer Indrė Šerpytytė's home may be a castle, a whitewashed pile near Inverness complete with crenellated battlements and a tower, but any expectations for a typical experience are shed on entry. Defying the tired logic of matching art contemporaneously to its surroundings, Šerpytytė has rejuvenated a centuries-old space, hanging its walls with contemporary pieces almost exclusively by women.

"Art is such a male arena," she says. "Work by men is so visible in galleries and on walls at home, and art by women is so easy to ignore. The castle is a Scottish castle, it's a very strong form, particularly outside, so David and I made a decision. Let's have this sensitivity of female artists inside."

She had a fair few at her disposal. Both Šerpytytė and her husband, David Roberts, are collectors of contemporary art, amassing more than 2,000 works including pieces by Phyllida Barlow, Rita Ackermann, Fiona Banner, Karla Black, and Anne Smith.

"We didn't say, let's pick the most expensive, the hottest artists of right now, we really delved into the archives to find what felt right. It gave us an opportunity to revisit pieces we bought fifteen, twenty years ago, bring them back into the light of day, and play with them. It was a chance to understand our journey of collecting through them."

The unconventional rehang was not without its challenges, not least working with the unwieldy architecture of an aging building more used to buttoned-up family portraits in hefty gold frames than the acid tones of Stella Vine's cigarette-wielding Kate Moss or the messy delicacy of a Phyllida Barlow chair hanging on the ballroom wall.

Šerpytytė, working with two assistants, completed the hanging project in three days. "I think it's really spruced up an old house. Older art, particularly portraits, is a lot about status, mortality, 'look at me,' and contemporary art is very different, it's about emotion, how we feel and how the artist feels about

the world. Joining the two together is very interesting, because they both speak of their time, but in very different ways. The mixture brings new energy into the house, and I love that."

This restorative energy is central to how the couple and their baby daughter, Constance, experience the house, as a refuge from London and an opportunity

to get closer to nature. "My studio is in London so this is a space to relax, have friends, not work, spend time with my daughter. There is something spiritual about Scotland. Nature is so strong here. It's a proper escape, a place to recharge."

However, Šerpytytė and Roberts's ever-expanding art collection—the garden is dotted with works predominantly by male artists such as Jeppe Hein—as well as a flourishing vegetable garden

holy water cannot help you now

and the river running by the front door,
means that weekends for twenty are not
infrequent. “It’s such a wonderful place
so we want to share it. People get so
excited because there is so much history
and so many things to see. It’s a really
big house, but it’s intimate, it’s very cozy
and doesn’t feel overwhelming.” Life in
a castle, surrounded by the traditional
trappings of wealth and family history,
inevitably prompts thoughts of heritage
and inheritance. For Šerpytytė,

her work hanging the house, sliding a
darkly irreverent collage of faces by
Cathy Lomax between two eighteenth-
century ladies gazing nonchalantly out
over their blouson sleeves, has made her
reconsider what she wants to save for
posterity and why. “Living in this house
has made me understand that inheritance
is part of how we control our legacy, and in
the moment it gives us a sense that we will live
forever. But we have a Karla Black, made using
makeup powder, that is essentially ephemeral—
it won’t last my lifetime, let alone my children’s.
What are we holding onto and why? It’s an
interesting conversation.”

MARGHERITA MISSONI

With one of the most familiar names in fashion, it is perhaps surprising that Margherita Missoni has chosen to take up residence in a small Italian town some 35 miles from Milan.

In fact, Varese is the Missoni family's hometown, where Margherita grew up. "I have very deep roots," she says. "I love the provincial, small-town life, and I think it's very healthy for children to grow up in this environment. It's a good contrast to fashion and all that glitter."

It helps that her husband, racing driver Eugenio Amos, also grew up in Varese so he understood its appeal. Not that it's hard to see. The Missoni-Amos house sits in a wealth of green overlooking Lake Varese, sloping gardens dipping into a forest, views extending to the Alps.

While the decision to move was an easy one, the process of building was hard. "I didn't realize it would be a full-time job," Missoni says. "It took four years. I don't know if I would do it again. Maybe I would buy a house that was ready-made—it's easier to live with someone else's mistakes than your own."

Working in collaboration with Cibic Workshop, the architecture studio founded by Memphis Group legend Aldo Cibic, the couple conceived a lofty wooden structure, a large family home that feels both grand and intimate, its rooms filled with light. "It's a very different house according to the seasons," says Missoni. "In the summer we're outside a lot, and in the winter, it's very cozy."

Part of the house's intimate feel comes from the pieces that fill it. "I have always kept my things," says Missoni. "I have stuff I bought in New York when I was twenty, which I took to Rome, to Milan, and now here. Also my husband and I love buying furniture together. While the house was being built, we went shopping—to flea markets abroad, to Salone del Mobile—finding special things and putting them in storage. Miraculously, it all fit."

Collecting, either for the house or for her work as creative director for M Missoni, is one of Margherita's great pleasures. "I really enjoy treasure hunting, whether it's a shop, a flea market, or online. It's how I relax."

1935 · 1947 · 1959 · 1971 · 1983 · 1995 · 2007 · SWINE
MONKEY
CERDO 1935 · 1947 · 1959 · 1971 · 1983 ·

1998 · 2010
1938 · 1950 · 1962 · 1986 · 1998

The spoils from these hunts are dotted throughout the house, alongside more recognizable pieces. A modernist sofa found on eBay and upholstered in blue velvet takes pride of place in the sitting room, where a Perspex screen by Andrea Branzi splits the space into two distinct areas. A curved cabinet bought in New York when Missoni was just twenty sits under her most prized possession, a large charcoal drawing by Mario Sironi that was a present from her grandfather.

The wooden four-poster in the master bedroom is by Mauro Mori, while the dining room has been transformed into a dreamily tonal forest with murals by Pictalab. The house is full of Missoni's collection of fake flowers that cover every surface, from the large enamel violet in one corner to the daisies that fill her office—"my favorite room in the house, the one that's only mine, although, because it's forbidden, my kids love coming in." Missoni is a brand associated with bright color and pattern, and Margherita's house is full of references to her heritage, some literal, some oblique. The drawing room's zodiac carpet is a Missoni prototype, taken directly from the showroom floor;

DE
VIOLETTE

chairs are covered in signature zigzags, but other pieces are more personal. “My mother and grandmother occasionally give things away, and if you’re there on the right occasion you get lucky,” she laughs. Treasures recovered from her grandmother’s storage unit include a sixties Murano glass chandelier and a parquet table salvaged from the royal waiting room in Stazione Milano Centrale. The luminous Giallo di Siena marble in the master bathroom is a nod to her grandmother’s Piero Portaluppi–designed Milan apartment where Margherita lived while at university. “As a family, we share a sensibility, and that’s a relaxing thing for us,” she explains. “We have a united aesthetic and a taste, then we all bring in our own times and life to add texture to our work. When I work now, I don’t need to ask, ‘Is it the right thing?’; I know what I like is Missoni.”

INDIA

SI · 405378

MARTINI RACING

Portia Alen-Buckley & Mike Lindley

Portia Alen-Buckley's house in Marrakech has a personal history. "The house belonged to Alain Mertens, who was a fabulous interior designer and my godfather," she says. "He left it to me in his will."

The bequest was a total surprise: a reflection, Alen-Buckley says, of her close bond with her godfather but also of his love for her mother, Gianni. "They met when he gave her a job at his shop on Beauchamp Place when she was sixteen. That's why he left it to me, it's really a testament to their relationship, they were best friends."

It was clear to Alen-Buckley from the outset that she did not want to make any radical alterations to the *riad*. "I love it how it is. I couldn't do a better job," she says. "The aesthetic feels very aligned to my aesthetic, which is because my mum grew up with Alain, and she has passed it on to me. It's all so closely knit."

Portia and her husband, Michael, first came to the house just after their wedding in 2017, a few months after Mertens passed away. "It was crazy hot—no one lives in Marrakech in August—so we were just alone. It made me feel very happy about it all, because it's so surreal when someone dies. It was so nice to spend some time there, meet his friends who worked for him, feel our way, and get a sense of the place."

They spent their six weeks at the house cowriting their first feature. "Now, two years on, we're making it. The house is part of the journey of our film, it's so sweet that it happened there." Tucked down an alleyway in the heart of Marrakech's medina, the riad is an oasis amid the hustle and bustle of one of the city's busiest quarters. Arched doorways lead off the riad's plant-filled central courtyard into various nooks for sitting and reading, for working, for eating, for sleeping.

"Alain restored the whole place, cultivating this effortless combination of traditional colors and contemporary European pieces, creating a fresh take on a traditional, heritage vibe. It's so uncluttered, but he has lots of objects everywhere, perfect objects."

Treasures include carved wooden masks, richly embroidered tapestries, delicate bobbin chairs, and copies of pieces by Cy Twombly and Andy Warhol that Mertens had bought in New York in the seventies. A favorite room is the library, which brings together nineteenth-century paintings, exquisite inlaid tables, teetering piles of books, and two iconic mid-century modern chairs by Eileen Gray and Ray and Charles Eames.

The roof comes into its own in the early evening. "When you go up around sunset some kind of insects come out, and all these little swallows start going berserk, hundreds of them

MARR

AKECH

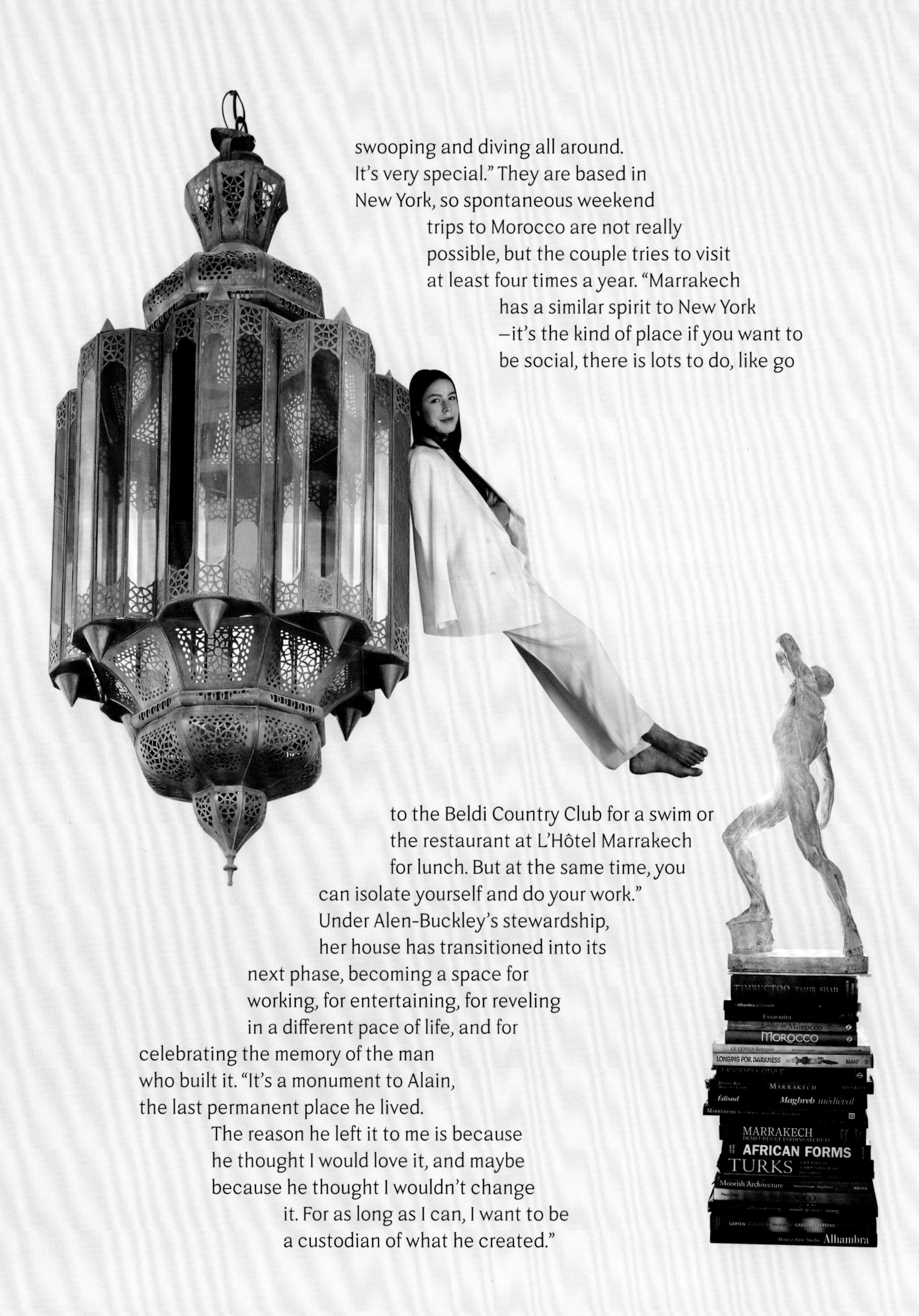

swooping and diving all around. It's very special." They are based in New York, so spontaneous weekend trips to Morocco are not really possible, but the couple tries to visit at least four times a year. "Marrakech has a similar spirit to New York —it's the kind of place if you want to be social, there is lots to do, like go to the Beldi Country Club for a swim or the restaurant at L'Hôtel Marrakech for lunch. But at the same time, you can isolate yourself and do your work." Under Alen-Buckley's stewardship, her house has transitioned into its next phase, becoming a space for working, for entertaining, for reveling in a different pace of life, and for celebrating the memory of the man who built it. "It's a monument to Alain, the last permanent place he lived. The reason he left it to me is because he thought I would love it, and maybe because he thought I wouldn't change it. For as long as I can, I want to be a custodian of what he created."

HAVE NO
FEAR
ZACHARY ARMSTRONG
ZACHARY ARMSTRONG

Stefan Simchowitz

Art dealer and consultant Stefan Simchowitz sets out his stall right away. "I am not having a bourgeois discussion about the mythologies of collecting," he declares. "The work I have is not passively bought, it's work acquired through a complex set of interactions I've had with people, primarily artists, so it's a constant language, a communication of community that occurs within the home."

Simchowitz's home is in Los Angeles' Carthay Circle, near Beverly Hills, and his office is across the street. "It really is a live/work situation. I have absolutely no separation between living and work."

He shares his home with his "partner in life, love, and business," Rosi Riedl, and their son, Morris—"he has no second name"—but the door is always open to visitors. "The house is really about people. We cook four times a week, we have a Friday night dinner for Shabbat. My home functions like a kibbutz where culture is the output. I think the element of public living improves my family life, it constantly brings new people into it, we're constantly engaging with new energy, new voices, building community."

He will not talk about favorite works—"I don't choose special pieces, everything is special that I buy"—but, in fairness, it would be hard to pick a highlight from his art-packed home. A bear in a tutu by Marnie Weber stands in the corner of the sitting room opposite a Marc Horowitz painting, while various "potions" by L occupy the floor and table. Two digital abstracts by Petra Cortright face off with a nude by Jonathan Edelhuber and an installation by Tyler Macko, titled—and demonstrably—*Bag of Oranges*. Another Edelhuber, a distressed painted quilt, covers the bed.

"My experience is mostly contemporary art," he says. "I live in these times—I live in the twenty-first century, not the eighteenth century."

Born in Johannesburg, Simchowitz entered the art world after studying economics at Stanford, spending a decade in the movie business—where he helped produce a cluster of films including *Requiem for a Dream*—and cofounding a photo service that went on to be sold to Getty Images.

"I got into art because I love great things," Simchowitz says. "I'm an aesthete —I've always loved things that are excellent, whether it's tables, chairs, artworks, clothing, literature, or ideas."

Today he encourages and supports young artists, buys their work and sells it on to his network of collectors who range from Hollywood actors and poker players to sports stars and billionaires. The roster of artists with whom he has worked—Sterling Ruby, Tauba Auerbach, Oscar Murillo, Amalia Ulman, Parker Ito, and Petra Cortright, among many others—reads as a who's who of contemporary talent, particularly post-Internet artists.

"I think of art as content. Social-media platforms enable art to go through this amazing transference where it starts functioning in the same way as TV or music—it has a content function as well as a physical function."

He views his role—which includes sidestepping galleries completely and buying and selling through Instagram—as remedying the inherent imbalance of the current system. "All I see out there are amazing artists who have no access to capital and very little chance of doing anything with a gallery because the gallery risks so much by representing artists who don't come from the right place, with the right degree. Exclusion is systematic and has to be stamped out."

His methods are controversial, seeing him disparaged, blacklisted, and dismissed by many establishment figures, but Simchowitz is optimistic that with time his methods will win out.

"I think you change things with repetition, and with communication, survival, conversation, and time, we can wear it down. It's like Muhammad Ali fighting George Foreman in Zaire in 1974. You take the punches, you use the ropes, you try not to get knocked out, until they're so tired they can't lift their hands anymore and then boom, you take them out. That's the strategy."

In the meantime, Simchowitz's Los Angeles home remains an incubator for his radical vision for the future of art dealing and living. "I take great pleasure that my place is somewhere people gather. I take pleasure in the fact I can share it with people. At the end of the day we are a community of people, and people enliven spaces—the art is just there as a medium of energy through which people can interact."

DWR 1
DWR 2
DWR 3
DWR 4
DWR 5
DWR 6
DWR 7
DWR 8
DWR 9
DWR 10
DWR 11
DWR 12

KEA

Adam Lippes

"I collect furniture constantly," announces fashion designer Adam Lippes. "I don't look at fashion, I look at furniture and objects and things."

His passion is evident from the doorway of the Brooklyn Heights apartment he shares with his boyfriend, Alexander Farnsworth, and their two labradoodles. Housed in a historic piece of New York real estate—"this is considered the most important house in Brooklyn," Lippes says—his extraordinary collection of art, furniture, and ornaments is matched only by the apartment's stellar views out over the East River.

The house's history dates back to the beginning of Brooklyn Heights itself. It was built by, and home to, the borough's first major developer, Hezekiah Pierrepont, and is today the starting point for walking tours of the area.

"I watch real estate obsessively," says Lippes, "and when I heard that this apartment was coming up I began a yearlong wooing of the owner, sending notes, gifting sweaters, taking tea with him and his girlfriend, persuading him to let me have it, restore it, take care of it."

The campaign was a success, and Lippes arrived in 2016, bringing an initially reluctant Farnsworth with him. "He was worried he was too young for Brooklyn," Lippes says. "Now I can't imagine living anywhere else," Farnsworth admits. "It's the West Village on steroids but without the tourists. It feels like you're walking through a movie set; it's incredible."

Lippes grew up in an aesthetically minded household—"my mother was an interior designer; my father was a huge collector"—but credits Oscar de la Renta with refining his taste. He worked with the designer for ten years, designing the brand's stores in Europe and Asia, becoming creative director at just twenty-seven. "Oscar was a second father to me. We traveled everywhere, visiting the greatest houses in the world, staying with all his fancy friends. It was incredible and eye-opening, it had a huge effect on me."

Lippes began collecting early on—"in my twenties I was collecting a lot of art, because at the time good English furniture was too expensive but

BROO
HEIG

KLYN
HTS

you could buy a good artist for $10,000. Then suddenly the art world became madly expensive so I switched to furniture."

The eclectic mix on show in Brooklyn Heights speaks to Lippes's magpie eye. Farrow & Ball's Setting Plaster is a consistent backdrop throughout, dotted with pieces by the likes of Pieter Schoolwerth, Eric Fischl, and Alex Katz—the latter a present from Lippes's father. The television room is covered from the twin banquette sofas to canopied ceiling in moody florals, lit by a decadently fringed lamp. The master bedroom is dominated by a chinoiserie-inspired four-poster bed, handmade in India. To one side is a wall of books, to the other a screen inherited from his mother, overlooked by a pyramid of eighteenth-century Chinese parrots topped off with a twenty-first-century seagull—"because we're on the water," shrugs Lippes.

He works from a desk in the drawing room, the Statue of Liberty visible through the trees. Farnsworth's office is on the other side of the house, from where he spots tour groups staring up at the historic facade.

"Ultimately the best of design for me is all about the mix," Lippes says. "Clothing is the same. And you either know how to do it or you don't. Decorating and design is like a good dinner party. I don't care what you're serving, or where it is, if you have the greatest mix of people from old to young to rich to poor to finance and art, it's going to be fun."

EGON SCHIELE
FC/T 306
KATE MOSS BY MARIO TESTINO
AROUND THAT TIME
HORST AT HOME IN VOGUE
JACQUES GRANGE INTERIORS
THE INTERIORS OF CHESTER JONES
LANDFORM BUILDING
LOUIS VUITTON

JANE KELTNER DE VALLE & GIANCARLO VALLE

Born and raised in Manhattan, Jane Keltner de Valle did not take the step of leaving the island lightly. "It was a huge move for me," she says. "Initially I wasn't interested in Brooklyn at all, but then I came to DUMBO and fell in love. There was a grittiness to it, I liked the old industrial buildings that had history and weren't just new builds, I liked the cobblestone streets, the atmosphere, the genuine community feeling. Now I'm a total Brooklyn evangelist."

It's easy to see why. Together with her husband, the architect and designer Giancarlo Valle, and their children, Roman (six) and Paloma (two), Keltner de Valle lives in a glass-fronted apartment in one of DUMBO's most famous buildings, a former cardboard factory built by Robert Gair on the banks of the East River. Also known as the Clocktower, its wall of windows offers a staggering view of Manhattan and its jumble of skyscrapers including One World Trade Center, home to Architectural Digest and Style Director Keltner de Valle's office.

The family moved into the building in 2014, when Roman was just one and while Valle was transitioning from architecture to interiors and furniture design. "This project was an incubator for all the new ideas I was having," he says, and his designs dot the apartment, from his smile chair in the sitting room to the wall-mounted lamp that swoops low—or high, it is adjustable—over the large maple dining table, another Valle original. Surveying the space, he says, "You can tell what's mine. It's an homage to Donald Judd, with a little bit of a twist." The minimalist master's influence is expressed most clearly in the kitchen, which centers on a colossal marble island attended by three tall pine chairs, their backs adorned with a ripple. This wave effect is echoed in the dark red screen in the sitting room, which Valle has used to frame the large windows. Naturally, the house operates not just as an incubator, but also as a showroom. "Friends come in and comment, and we do sell stuff as seen in the house," Valle says. "For everything else I have an official space on Canal Street." Of course, the house is not just a showcase for Valle's work, but also a celebration of the couple's shared interest in the worlds of art and design. Valle works from a Pierre Jeanneret desk, tucked in a book-lined corner nook at the end of the sitting room,

facing a Jayson Musson print, with a heavyset Ethiopian wooden armchair —partial inspiration for the Smile design— nearby. In the den, a marble coffee table by Gae Aulenti is overlooked by a painting by Katherine Keltner, Jane's sister, and a number of African masks.

"The masks are funny," Valle says. "My dad used to collect masks from southern Africa, and we had a lot of African art and primitive art growing up. I just rediscovered them recently and started picking them up myself. Obviously the kids love them."

The genius of the Valle household is its balance of Judd-esque simplicity and a playful, family-friendly spirit. For Roman and Paloma's bedroom, painted vivid Farrow & Ball blue, Valle created functional concealed storage using the ripple motif from the sitting room, as well as a simple plywood bed frame for his son. The couple added a salmon-hued canopy, attended by a menagerie of giraffe toys and a lion's head.

The canopy was not simply a design flourish, but a solution to an unexpected problem. "I thought it would be fun to have a feng shui expert come in and give us ideas about furniture arrangement or colors," Keltner de Valle explains. "It turns out this apartment has terrible feng shui because all our beds are under exposed beams. He wanted us to drop the ceilings, which would mean losing three feet of room height, so we were wracking our brains for more creative solutions. That's how we came up with the canopies, which I love so much and bring me so much joy, but part of me wishes we hadn't asked him to come."

The canopy in the Valles's bedroom is a simple white affair, part of a muted color scheme featuring cement walls, a neutral Facett sofa, a rust silk tapestry, and a minimalist teak desk. What captures the attention are the portraits of the children, two jaw-dropping photographs by the artist Marilyn Minter, taken when Roman and Paloma were each eight months old.

Minter is a client of Valle's—he worked on the renovation of her house in upstate New York—and the images result from her technique of shooting through glass, spraying it with water and using ice to create a singular effect of fog and drips. "She's a fascinating late-career artist, New York based, a contemporary of Cindy Sherman and Laurie Simmons," says Keltner de Valle. "We don't know how the kids will feel about them when they're older, but we thought they were cool things for them to inherit one day."

YOLANDA EDWARDS

If you take a car out of New York City and drive northwest for a couple of hours, you may find yourself in a hamlet in Sullivan County. Head deep into the woods, and if you are lucky, you will catch a glimpse of a gleaming white box overlooking a field rippling with monarch butterfly caterpillars, a haze of smoke rising from a barbecue, a bare-legged woman building log piles in the woods nearby.

This is the upstate home of Yolanda Edwards, Matt Hranek—alumni of *Condé Nast Traveler* and editors of, respectively, *YOLO Journal* and *Wm Brown*—and their daughter, Clara, a prefab house designed by Austrian architect Oskar Leo Kaufmann in his first-ever US commission.

"Before, we were living in a cedar cabin at the end of the meadow with just a Japanese soaking tub, a Weber grill, and a coffeepot," remembers Hranek. "Then Yolanda got pregnant, I met Oskar, and I asked him if he could design something for us. He said, 'Come to Austria and we'll figure it out.' So we went, fell in love with everything they were doing, and designed the house totally à la carte."

The resulting structure cost $250,000 and arrived in five shipping containers around the same time as Clara. It took four days to erect and is a master class in clean lines and clarity of vision. "It was always our intention to build a minimalist space for living that was about modesty," says Hranek. "Whenever I got overexcited, Yolanda would keep me pulled back. She'd say a guest needs a hook, and a shelf, and maybe a chair. Nothing more."

The tone is classic. European oak veneers cover the walls and ceiling, the table, island, and built-ins were made by Heinz Rüscher—who works with Peter Zumthor—while the daybed and twin beds in Clara's room are by Hans Wegner. The chairs and side table were made for IBM, original pieces that Hranek found in his hometown of Binghamton, where the company had its early offices.

"We love the rush of thrifting, we love the hunt," says Edwards. "We like to see it and touch it and talk about it together. That's what makes an interesting house—people taking their time and filling it with a lifetime of finds and souvenirs." Their skill as collectors and designers is in keeping the connecting thread between object and place. A wall of antlers is a nod to the upstate New York tradition of game hunting, opposite sit two paintings by Native American artists, while the muted floral cushions are by New York designer Judy Ross. But the star of the house is indisputably its wall of 40-foot windows. "For us, the art is outside," says Hranek, "that's why there's very little on the walls. I don't like distractions, that's why we don't need a television—we can just watch everything unfold outside, watch the world changing over the course of the day."

"This is not our daily life, it's our weekend," says Edwards. "The Wi-Fi is terrible, so instead of working I'll go into the woods and pick up logs and make stacks. Matt goes to the farmer's market and makes incredible food. I love the lack of things to do; we just think about what we're going to make for the next meal. It's a reconnection, a slowing down of life."

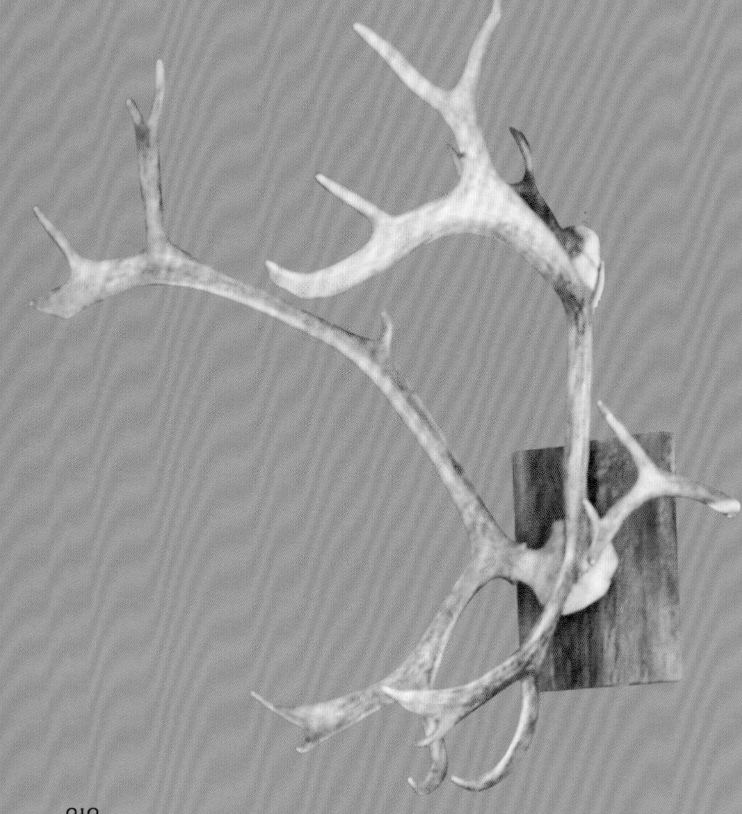

FORAGED FLORA

HELMUT NEWTON
HIDE AND SEEK
RIPAILLES
COOKING

CORDON ROUGE

FREMONT CENTER
HANKINS
DELAWARE RIVER

SAMUEL ROSS

The home Samuel Ross has created with his wife, Jennifer, and their daughter, Genesis, is more than just a dwelling. "It's an expression of our value system," he says. "We believe it is important to have objects around us that emanate a sense of aspiration, almost a code to hold oneself accountable to. It's about showing people that you've made a concise choice about what will inhabit the space you live in."

Ross is the multi-award-winning designer behind A-Cold-Wall and one of the most significant voices to emerge on London's fashion scene in the past decade. His label is rooted in streetwear, the story of growing up between Northamptonshire and Brixton told through product and design, a spirit that has morphed as the designer has matured. "Our latest collection was luxury Italian-milled, London-pattern menswear," he laughs. "Most of the headlines said, 'Samuel Ross doesn't make streetwear anymore.'"

Just as his design mentality has changed for his line, so too has it changed for his home. "We started off as brutalists in an industrial warehouse that was all steel, cement, and concrete sculptures with harsh 90-degree edges," Ross says. "Then you have a child and you change your whole psyche on what a house should be and what it should look and feel like."

The family moved to a four-story East London town house and embraced a whole new design ethos of color, space, and soft form that serves "almost as an incubator for Genesis, to keep her mind stimulated."

However, the removal of sharp edges and the addition of bright color did not dilute the rigor of Ross's aesthetic. The chairs are mostly design classics by the likes of Ron Arad, Mies van der Rohe, and Ray and Charles Eames, the couple picked the Kvadrat fabric for their HAY sofa right down to the Pantone shade and grams per square meter, while the beaming flower cushions on the sofa were a present from the artist Takashi Murakami. Artworks by the African-American artist Kerry James Marshall lean against the white walls, while a piece by Daniel Arsham, a friend of Ross's, sits near a family portrait.

PLACES AND SPACES I'VE BEEN

"We don't need a lot of stuff," says Ross. "Recently I threw away about 450 objects because I just don't need them. My job is to design the future, not to consume. The idea of the home should be a temple and shrine to ideation and family."

The evolution of Ross's idea of home and space is taking yet another new shape in the coming months when the family moves to Northamptonshire, into a twenty-room manor house in the countryside where he will spend half the week.

"I was born in London and spent my childhood coming down from the country to visit family in Brixton, so I've always had a duality of complete countryside and intense city. London doesn't facilitate the type of family life we envisage, which has a focus on fresh produce and agriculture, on interacting and engaging with nature, a more peaceful and balanced upbringing for our daughter. I love this city, but what I see in it now isn't what I believe the future is. I think that to manifest the future, one needs physical and mental space."

So what will be taken to the new house and what will be left behind? Ross's thirst for total minimalism is tempered by those pieces with something approaching sentimental value. "A lot of the sculpture was made by Jennifer and me, and the blue rock is by me. It represents a time in my history when I started to delve into sculpture and installation, hence why it's there. These are objects that belong to the family, that are not just there to take up space, but that represent a moment in one's career." Ross's home is an exercise in intellectual domesticity, in the expression of a value system through design and form with every detail considered and questioned.

"I collect chairs because I find the form so interesting," he says. "Chairs are really good at transforming a space, and they reveal so much about someone's taste and interests. It's interesting how these little nuances produce codes that people are able to pick up on. Each chair has its own persona, and I like to think each one reflects a type of open-mindedness that we hold as a family."

RICARD
RICARD
PORTOBELLO ROAD
GIN
MARTINI
EXTRA DRY

Beata Heuman

Beata Heuman is known for her highly individual aesthetic that has taken her from Nicky Haslam's practice to becoming one of London's most in-demand interior designers. With at least eight or nine projects running at any one time, ranging from residential homes to restaurants to her own line of fabrics and furniture, the complete redecoration of a West London house for herself and her growing family could have seemed overwhelming.

"Lots of designers say designing for themselves is more difficult, but I don't agree," she says. "I prefer not having someone I need to answer to, and it's so satisfying to be able to complete something over time, finding or making the perfect things."

Heuman's style is a blend of her pared-back Scandinavian heritage, irreverence and courage from Haslam, and Italian joie de vivre inculcated in Florence. "I've worked out my look now. It's sometimes grand, it's clean, it always has a sense of humor."

Beata and her husband, John Finlay, moved into the house in late 2016 and have since been joined by their daughters, Gurli and Alma. "It isn't very big, which is really satisfying in that we do actually use the whole house," Heuman says. "But with children running around, and my aesthetic being so colorful with a lot of things going on, keeping it tidy is very important."

In Heuman terms, "tidy" is code for ingenious, her space-saving measures always the height of elegance. The fridge is stowed within a bespoke armoire, handcrafted by Alfred Newall of The London Workshop, while simple chests of drawers extend deep into the walls for extra storage.

But a home is so much more than its practicalities, and it is in the joyful details that Heuman's vision is most apparent. The kitchen's glass and brass ceiling was inspired by nineteenth-century Viennese patisseries and brings height and light into a narrow space. Creatures are everywhere, prowling across the flag that sits above the sitting room mantelpiece, curved around mirrors in the dining room, draped across the spare bed. The children's bedroom is a re-creation of the famous Bemelmans mural from New York City's Carlyle Hotel, made bespoke for Gurli and Alma with depictions of rabbits and the Hammersmith Bridge.

LUCIAN FREUD PORTRAITS
NPG
FLORES-VIANNA HAUTE BOHEMIANS
VENDOME
Thierry Coudert
Beautiful People of the Café Society
Flammarion

"I like transporting people into another world, a made-up world," Heuman says. "It's quite childish, I suppose, but there's something about it I find very alluring, exciting, fun, playful, and a bit strange. It's the same with the art. You can easily tell who it belongs to. Anything that's a little bit weird and creepy is me."

Another recurring motif is perhaps less expected. "I love the Michelin Man," she smiles. "He is everywhere. I think he is really well designed. When I make bespoke pieces I add lots of curves, swirls, and waves because that's often what you need in a room. Something with movement."

With the project complete, it would be understandable if the inveterate creative in Heuman was already getting itchy feet, but she believes leaving the house would be impossible.

"I would be too sad to leave the kitchen ceiling," she says. "We talked about it for so long, it was so expensive, it's so glamorous, and it will actually stay that way as it's out of the reach of children's prying hands."

MARC JACOBS
BYREDO PARFUMS
LA TULIPE

Visitors to Will Cooper's East Village apartment in New York City might be initially surprised by what they find.

As the creative director of ASH NYC, and the man responsible for the aesthetic of the company's three hotels in New Orleans, Detroit, and Providence, designer Cooper is associated with a hedonistic blend of color, pattern, and texture.

However, he says, "I have to live in white. I have to come back to serenity in my home; otherwise it's chaos in my mind."

But he also admits this is probably just a phase. Cooper has been in his apartment for four years, and during that time it has taken on a number of different guises. "I use my home as a laboratory," he says, "moving through ideas, thinking about color in a space. We painted the bedroom in yellow as an experiment for Baltimore, but it was too intense. I slept in it twice before getting rid of it."

The apartment's current state is profoundly Zen, an all-white retreat with clean, industrial light fittings and a tightly edited selection of mostly monochromatic art and objects. "The overarching idea was palate-cleansing and white, cleaning up all that chaos from the previous version of the apartment. I feel like everybody's apartments are full of things, and that makes me claustrophobic. This was about creating a really tight vision that is also comfortable."

The living room is a triumph of minimalism, white all over from the long banquette that runs along the window wall and the slip-covered chairs to the Robert Sonneman floor lamps, the marble coffee table, and Luca Pancrazzi's dreamy cloudscape facing off with the mirror.

"I wanted cleanliness but also soul," Cooper says, "and you see a bit of soul with the Donghia chair legs visible under the cover, the skirt on the banquette that adds a little decorator flair. It's simplicity but there are a lot of interesting references."

The bedroom is the definition of pared back, its parameters demarcated using a mirrored screen and an antique desk. On the walls are contemporary pieces by Mel Bochner, Mara de Luca, and Aleksandar Duravcevic.

Connections and references proliferate throughout the space, demonstrating Cooper's concise vision. Pancrazzi started his career as arte povera pioneer Alighiero Boetti's studio assistant, and one of Boetti's iconic embroideries hangs near Pancrazzi's larger canvas.

"Art really has a special energy, and there has to be something personal and, for me, something narrative when using it in an interior," says Cooper. "I don't want anything that I don't see eye to eye with, because it's challenging. If there's one too many things, then it's claustrophobic."

Every object has meaning. The cluster of ceramics on the coffee table is a memento of his time working on the Siren hotel. "With every project I try to bring something back. These are by a collective of crazy ceramicists from Detroit called Hamtramck Ceramck, and these are the most demure and refined pieces they had."

With the next project already on the horizon, Cooper is resigned about how long the current environment will last. "As soon as I moved in here four years ago, I wanted it to be all white. I've been working towards this for all that time, finding a way to execute it, figuring out what it would look like. But I'm a chameleon. I like this look, but I also like gingham and black and I really like it all tight. That allows me to work out all these fantasies in my own home."

the complete works
BENJAMIN BALDWIN
ARCHITECTURAL DIGEST COUNTRY HOMES
Todd Eberle Empire of Space
The World of Madeleine Castaing

BAZAAR 150 YEARS
PERROTIN
DREAM TEAM
the complete works
THE ART BOOK
TASCHEN'S PARIS Hotels, Restaurants & Shops
HOPPER
VLADIMIR KAGAN
bauhaus
Jean Royère
Jean Royère
THE INTERNATIONAL BOOK OF LOFTS
LE CORBUSIER
NORBERT WOLF
ART DECO
CHASING BEAUTY RICHARD PHIBBS
AMERICAN ORIGINALS
R.S.V.P.
BENJAMIN BALDWIN: An Autobiography in Design
NEW YORK INTERIORS
ANNIE LEIBOVITZ
TASCHEN

JEN RUBIO

There is a sticker on the back of the front door to Jen Rubio's apartment. "It was here when I moved in," she says. "It reads, 'A Better Place is Hard to Find,' and we can't get it off. It's stuck there. It feels like an omen."

Rubio had been planning her perfect New York apartment ever since she moved to the city in 2011. "Obviously my first apartment was tiny, but I always thought, 'One day I'm going to have a big place full of my stuff, and it will be my sanctuary.'"

Eighteen months ago she found it, an airy, open-plan space in the center of SoHo where she now lives with her cockapoo puppy, Bizzy.

Rubio has an intensely focused and structured office life. "With work, everything is planned, and everything has to have a reason. So when it comes to my apartment, it's what makes me happy and no one else. I don't care if things match, I just care if I love it."

She created a blank canvas, covering up a brick wall—"You know how New Yorkers love exposed brick? I don't. So, we had it covered and painted white. Everyone thought I was crazy, but now the apartment feels way bigger"—and filling it with her favorite things either collected on trips abroad or bought at auction.

A David Hockney screen sits near the huge windows that gaze directly along a perpendicular street—"There are no other views like it in New York"—and a vast, velvet circular sofa surrounds an Yves Klein Blue table. A delicate mobile sculpture by Tomás Saraceno hangs in a corner, near a sketchily carved elephant Rubio rescued from a generic fate. "We went to a marble quarry in India, and that was the elephant before he had been fully chipped into detail," she recalls. "They thought I was crazy for trying to buy it, so they just gave it to me."

A wall of line drawings has an unexpected story. "I had just broken up with my boyfriend, and I went to see this woman in Vancouver who sketches you naked while you're talking—or in my case, crying. At the end of the twenty minutes, I was naked emotionally and physically and the whole floor was covered with sketches of my naked body. I picked the best one and got it

JET
BABY

couriered to his office." It all ended well. The couple reconciled—they are now engaged—and Rubio framed six of the images and hung them in her living room. Her fiancé is also responsible for the Ed Ruscha that hangs over the fireplace. *Jet Baby* was the background wallpaper on my iPhone for about five years, and he knew how much I loved it so he bought it for my birthday."

Having at last created her New York sanctuary space, Rubio is reluctant to spend too much time away from it. "Now I never go out,"

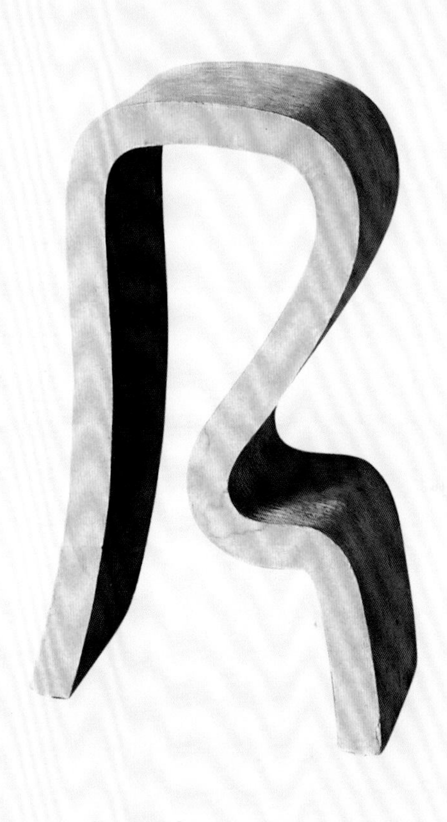

she says. "I always host people here. I don't have that many parties—board games sometimes, that's why I got the round sofa—but when I'm trying to recruit creative people I bring them here, because it's more my aesthetic. My office is two blocks away so I can always get there if I need to, but this is where I do my work, where I do my Peloton, where I relax, and no one can bother me."

PICASSO'S KITCHEN
MYKONOS MUSE
PORTRAITS
COMPORTA BLISS
VOLEZ VOGUEZ VOYAGEZ

CRAIG ROBINS

"I was living in Barcelona and I didn't have much money because I was a student, but my parents gave me a little bit and I bought a minor sketch by Salvador Dalí." So answers real estate innovator Craig Robins when asked what started his now extensive and extraordinary art collection.

"I had spent some time before that in Madrid and became fascinated by Goya, and I just loved the influence that Dalí, Miró, and Picasso had on Barcelona. That's what really got me interested in art."

Returning to his hometown of Miami, Robins pondered whether to become an art dealer or to go into the real estate business. "Being an art dealer seemed really impractical at that time in Miami, and the real estate business seemed kind of boring. But then I was really lucky because the redevelopment of South Beach was like merging my two interests. Working to rescue and renovate beautiful art deco buildings was a little bit like collecting sculptures."

Robins has continued to blend his passions, employing culture and commerce to reinvigorate not just neglected South Beach but also Miami's Design District, transforming them into globally renowned commercial centers dotted with luxury stores, famous restaurants, and site-specific artworks by his favorite artists and designers, including John Baldessari, Zaha Hadid, and Marc Newson. He worked with Sam Keller to bring Art Basel to Miami, confirming the city's status as so much more than a party town.

"When you combine the fun, the sex appeal, of Miami with the global cultural platform that the city has become, you get this very unusual appeal. That's what I love about Miami. It's fun but it's also very serious. Design, architecture, and art are advocated in our community."

They are certainly advocated in his extraordinary home. Robins has lived on the property in Sunset Islands for nearly two decades, but in the lead-up to his 2015 wedding to fellow real estate developer Jackie Soffer and the joining of their two families (the couple have three children each), they decided to expand.

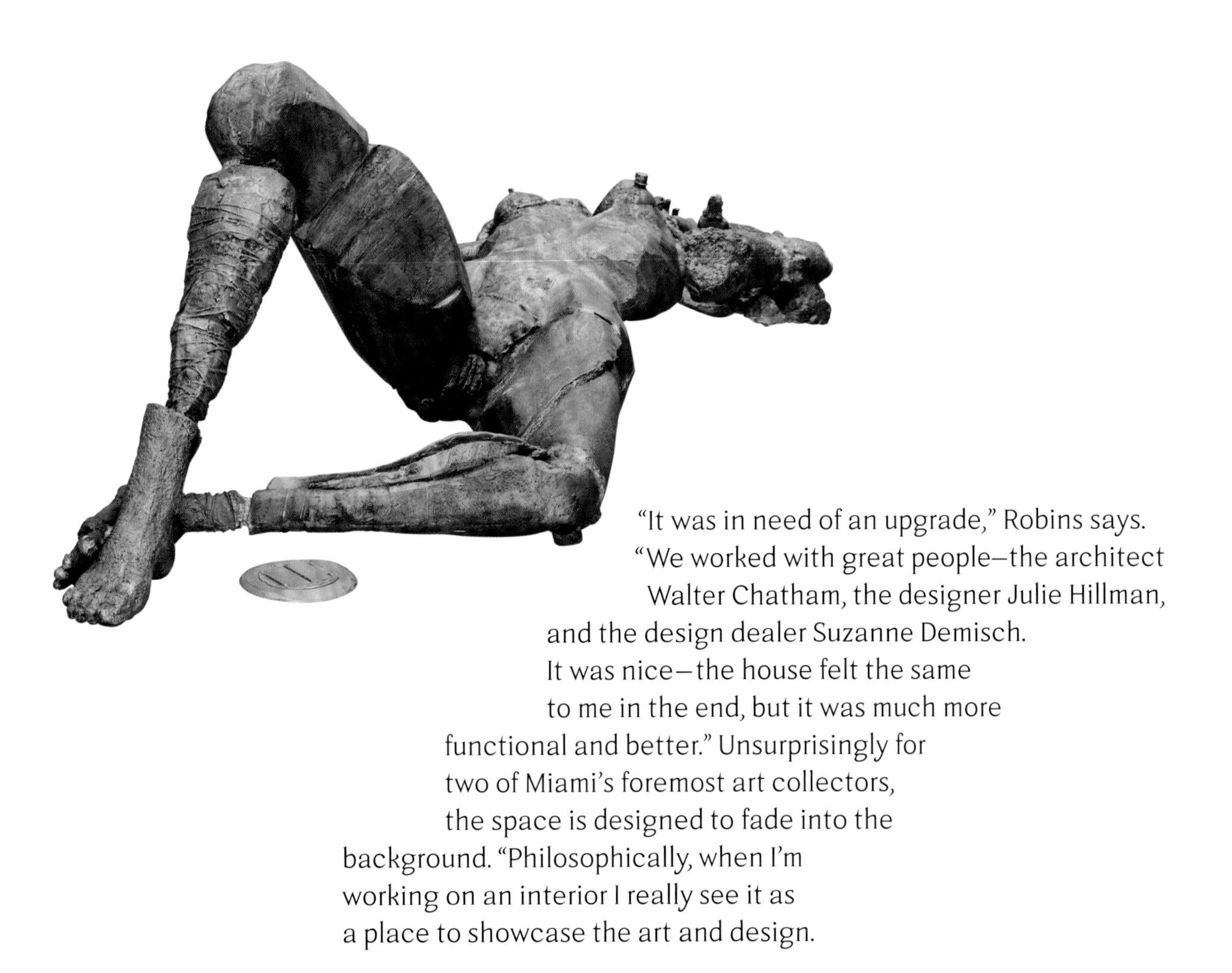

"It was in need of an upgrade," Robins says. "We worked with great people—the architect Walter Chatham, the designer Julie Hillman, and the design dealer Suzanne Demisch. It was nice—the house felt the same to me in the end, but it was much more functional and better." Unsurprisingly for two of Miami's foremost art collectors, the space is designed to fade into the background. "Philosophically, when I'm working on an interior I really see it as a place to showcase the art and design.

A clean white wall is all I need. We don't need a lot of decorative devices or fancy finishes—the art and design are what enrich the environment." The collection is truly jaw-dropping. The sitting room alone features works by John Baldessari and John Currin overlooking mid-century masterpieces by Charlotte Perriand and Gio Ponti, as well as a Marc Newson ladder and a Tom Dixon lamp. The curved dining table is by Zaha Hadid, as, in fact, is the entire master bathroom. "Zaha was a very close friend and when we were working on the house, my wife asked for her advice on the bathroom. Zaha, who was one of the most generous people I've ever known, said it might be a better idea if we had her design the whole thing. That's really my ultimate dream. To have something in our house that is such an important example of design."

A pavilion designed by David Adjaye for the entrance of Design Miami in 2011 sits in the garden. "It was so beautiful and so powerful that after the fair Jackie and I decided to acquire it. It's an incredible meditative place to go, either to socialize or to read or just sit and contemplate."

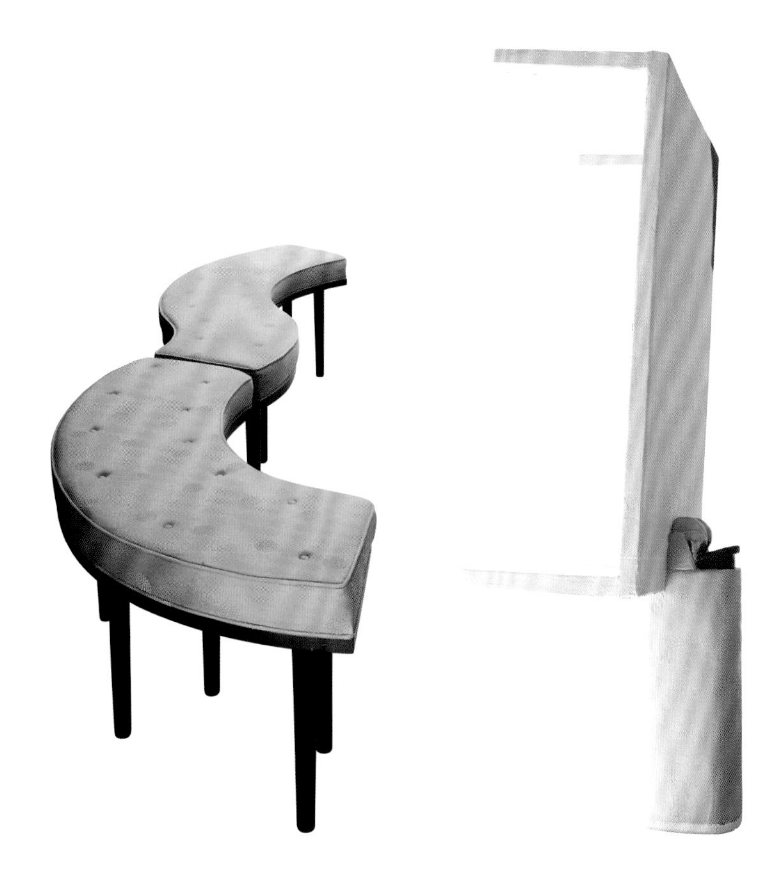

Robins's passion for collecting has seen him accumulate a lot of art, too much to exhibit at any one time. "I do have a lot in storage, but it goes in cycles. Certain art will be very relevant at one moment and less so at another point. So I like the idea—on a much smaller scale—of doing what museums do: installing different art, interacting with it for a period of time, then thinking about different things."

At home, as in his commercial projects, Robins believes that art has transformative power. "Living in a more creative environment inspires all of us and increases our happiness and our basic consciousness," he says. "Ultimately, I see art as a frontier from which mankind advances."

FRANCIS BACON

Kim Jones

Everyone knows Kim Jones. Formerly of Dunhill and Louis Vuitton, now creative director of Dior Menswear, he is a truly visionary designer, feted for his singular vision as well as his dynamic collaborations with the likes of KAWS, Raymond Pettibon, Shawn Stussy, and Supreme.

But his interests expand far beyond fashion. "I like lots of different things," he says with typical understatement, and his house in West London serves as a backdrop for his various collections that extend from Leigh Bowery clothes and Bloomsbury Group artworks to Antonio Lopez drawings and an astonishing library of rare and precious books.

A serene modernist gem, the house is tucked so subtly down a mews that no one would know it was there. "I had been looking for a big Georgian house to suit all my collections," Jones says, "but when I came here I just knew immediately. I had that feeling—it's so Zen, this house."

Designed by Gianni Botsford and built using metal, glass, and concrete, the house's huge rooms and high ceilings achieve a grandeur that never feels cold. Paintings, ceramics, and furniture by the Bloomsbury Group artists line the walls and shelves, the fruits of an obsession that started when Jones was growing up in Sussex, living near Charleston Farmhouse.

"I've been collecting Bloomsbury for years. The first pieces I bought were two Duncan Grant paintings, then I bought a Vanessa Bell cup on eBay and they pointed me to another seller for paintings. That's how I got into it, kind of by accident."

Now the collection is probably one of the best in the world, and it includes a child's desk painted by Duncan Grant for his and Vanessa Bell's daughter, Angelica, a Roger Fry screen that belonged to Evelyn Waugh and is mentioned at the start of *Brideshead Revisited*, photographs of Fry taken by Vanessa Bell, and a selection of rare books from the Bloomsbury Group's shelves.

"I've got the copy of *Orlando* that Virginia Woolf inscribed to Vita Sackville-West," Jones says, adding quickly, "It's in the safe, of course."

An upstairs office is lined with Vitra vitrines filled with pieces from Jones's exhaustive auction hunting. There are sketches by Leigh Bowery, Elizabeth Taylor's mask, a letter from Joan Crawford to Katharine Hepburn, Keith Haring's to-do lists, and a Lee Radziwill postcard from Peter Beard, while an abstract oil on the wall of the library turns out to be a self-portrait by Frank Sinatra, who briefly

took up painting on the advice of a therapist after his breakup with Ava Gardner. A group of Polaroids set in UV plastic on the table is by Araki. Ranks of ceramics are by, variously, Hylton Nel, Vanessa Bell, and Pablo Picasso. A Francis Bacon rug hangs in the vast sitting room. Works by Derek Jarman, Ryan McGinley, and René Magritte hang in the more intimate space of his bedroom. The garden furniture was originally in Yves Saint Laurent's villa in Marrakech. "People think I just like pop art," Jones muses. "I do like pop art. But I like so

LOCUSTS
FASHION NOW 2
DUST BOOK

many other things as well." Spread from floor to ceiling across a whole wall in his sitting room, Jones's library is his "big obsession." Housed on shelves built to a design by Jean Prouvé, it includes the only copy of *Studio 54* magazine ever printed, Arthur Rimbaud's *A Season in Hell* inscribed to Jones by his friend Kate Moss, a first edition of *On the Road*

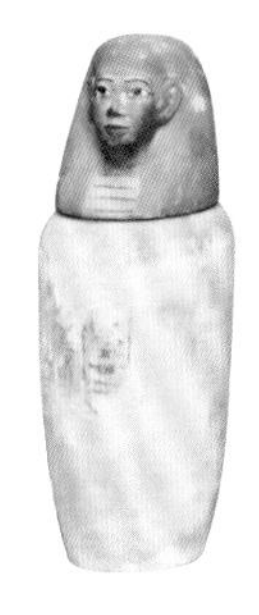

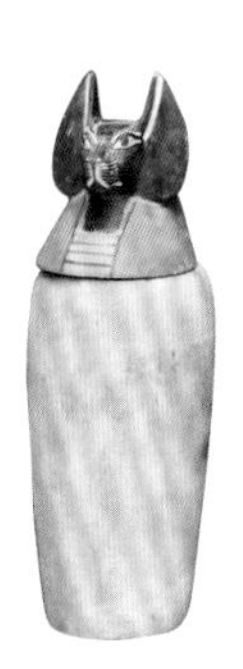

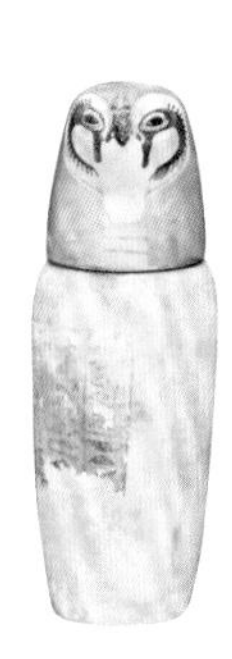

by Jack Kerouac, a preview copy of *Howl* by Allen Ginsberg, and a gallerist's copy of the catalogue for Andy Warhol's first major New York show. "I've started to order it properly," he says. "It's still a work in progress." The house marks Jones's permanent move back to London after eight years shuttling between the UK and Paris. "This feels like home forever," he says. "I think it's perfect. I love having everything in one place, to edit and take stock. I have everything I need." With his four dogs settled in—they particularly love the KAWS chair made of stuffed animals—his extraordinary art collection on the walls, and his library falling into place, it is hard to disagree.

Camilla Guinness

A friend's copy of the *Sunday Times*, brought to a lunch party in London, was the unconventional way Camilla Guinness and her late husband, Jasper, discovered their Tuscan farmhouse, Arniano.

"We were living in Florence at the time, so it was weird that we found our house in the back of an English newspaper," Camilla says. "But we'd been looking for months and getting nowhere. Estate agents kept taking us to places that had already been restored or were next to main roads."

But this is not a story of love at first sight. "Arniano wasn't what we were looking for at all. We wanted something much bigger, we wanted outbuildings, big trees, a loggia. It was just very surprising inside: so much light on the ground floor, these huge arched doorways and that view, it is simply unbelievable, so we gave up thoughts of anything else."

This was 1989; the couple had just discovered they were having a baby and needed to move out of Florence for some more space. But the task they gave themselves was formidable. "I wasn't an interior designer at all at the time," Camilla says. "The house was just a roof and floors. No electricity or anything. We did a lot ourselves. We painted everything, we laid a lot of stones, it was exciting."

The house and grounds became an incubator for both Guinnesses. Jasper transformed the garden—once just rubble and stony ground—into a verdant, cypress-tree-dotted utopia, establishing his reputation as a landscape architect in the process, while Camilla developed her signature blend of Italian and English style, of sophistication and comfort, of effervescent foreign finds and pared-back elegance.

"I'm definitely a scavenger," she says. "I sourced everything in the house myself, from shops and auctions around Italy, the big markets at Kempton and Newark, lots in France. I like finding things that I can then take out of context. I feel like everything is very suited to an Italian farmhouse without being something you've seen in an Italian farmhouse before."

A huge painted canvas hanging on the upstairs sitting room wall is the first thing the couple bought for the house: "we got it from Sotheby's in

Florence. It's so big that nobody wanted it, but I like how theatrical it is, and then everything else is a bit plain."

A wall hanging in the drawing room was a present to Jasper from his uncle Desmond Guinness, the founder of the Irish Georgian Society. "Desmond hung it in Castletown, the first house he saved for the Society, and it was there until 1992,

when he gave it to Jasper, who was his godson. It's such a lovely thing."

A set of dreamy murals in a bedroom are the work of Virginia Loughnan, an artist and friend who stayed with the family for a long time. "She moved to New York before the murals were done, so I got her to come back a few years later to finish them."

The different elements come together to form an intriguing hybrid. "Italian houses often aren't very comfortable," says Camilla. "They are design-led, not comfort-led. Arniano doesn't feel English, but it has the comfort, the coziness, of an English house. Also, I like lying down all the time, which is why most things are a daybed or a huge sofa." These days Camilla splits her time between Italy and London, spending

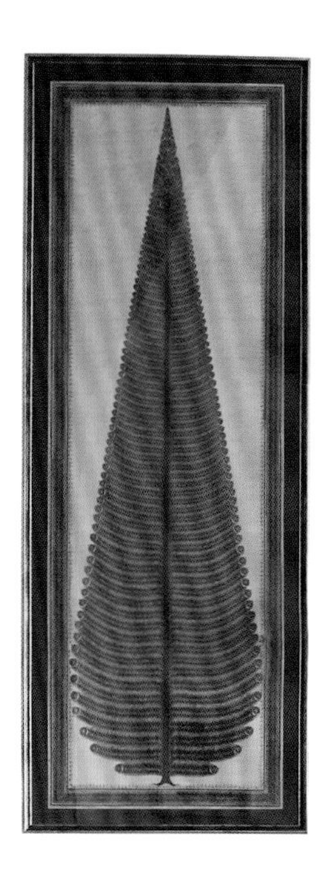

cGJ
MAY·1985
THE HISTORY OF WORLD SCULPTURE
THE GOLDEN BOUGH
THE LAST STUART QUEEN
THE GLORIOUS CONSTELLATIONS
GAMBERAIA
TUSCANY

five months of the year at Arniano. "I like it when it's cooler. It's a very nice winter house, it's really cozy." In the summer her elder daughter, Amber, and her friend Will Roper-Curzon host weeklong painting courses, opening Arniano's doors to enthusiastic amateur artists. "It's been great and people just love it," Camilla reports. "It keeps it all vibrant."

This new tide of guests are voluble fans of Camilla's unique way with interiors. "People feel very comfortable at Arniano, and someone explained it was because you can sit down virtually anywhere and have a conversation. I do think about that a lot, how far away someone is sitting when you're talking to them, can you put a drink down. I'm not terribly social myself, but I like creating a comfortable atmosphere for people to chat."

ROSETTA GETTY

With one of the most famous surnames in the world, it is not surprising that top of the list of requirements for fashion designer Rosetta Getty's house were "peace and privacy."

"I also wanted something unique," she says. "When we found this bright pink 1920s Spanish-style hacienda, with huge gardens and incredible views of the hills, it ticked every box."

Key to the house's perfection was the on-site recording studio for Rosetta's husband, actor and musician Balthazar, and enough wall and floor space for the couple's extensive contemporary art collection. "I have been collecting since my early twenties," says Rosetta. "The first piece I bought was by Robert Motherwell, and now I focus on work by young female artists, LA artists, and of course my children—I've kept all their drawings and paintings from over the years, and they are priceless."

This answer speaks to the reality of the Getty home, which is furnished with staggering works of art yet designed for down-to-earth family life with Balthazar and Rosetta's four children, Cassius, Grace, Violet, and June. "No matter how busy everyone is, I try to make sure that we all eat dinner together every night," Rosetta says. "We also love entertaining, so friends and family come over most weekends for a thing we call Soul Food Sundays."

This is a house where great art and design are celebrated, admired, but also used. The reading lamp in the library is by Isamu Noguchi, a spiderlike table by Michael Wilson hosts a leafy plant, and the mandatory family suppers are held at a dining table and chairs by the mid-century legend Jacob Kjaer.

One ballroom-sized space evokes a gallery atmosphere being furnished almost entirely with art, the majority by female artists. One of Olympia Scarry's *Licks,* a luminous column of Himalayan salt cubes, stands near a sprawling Hayden Dunham sculpture strung from the ceiling on chains. However, the serenity can be dashed in a moment should one of the children take the opportunity to play the grand piano, as they frequently do.

Just next door in the library, the atmosphere is all coziness and calm, from the vintage rugs on the floor and the shelves crammed with books,

HARING
ELLIOTT ERWITT'S KOLOR
MARIO TESTINO
IN YOUR FACE
VENETIAN
CITIES OF DESTINY
Oriental Carpets
HOUSE
Cabinet of
BRASSAI
MURDOCH
THE READER
PILGRIMS OF THE NIGHT
THE SECOND MIRACLE
HIP HOTELS

LA

the battered leather armchair by Illum Wikkelso and Rosetta's favorite piece of furniture in the house, the Charlotte Perriand and Jean Prouvé daybed. "This is my sanctuary," says Rosetta. "It's where I gather my thoughts and get inspired." The joy of living in LA is the constant lure of the outdoors, and the Getty house celebrates this both in its lush gardens, fern-lined balcony, and idyllic cacti-lined pool area, and inside too. There is greenery everywhere, in corner nooks, on the piano, lined up along the windowsills. "I really love plants," smiles Getty. "In fact, our dining room has actual living vines that have grown

along the ceiling and the walls." Offering peace and privacy, space and intimacy, business and art, nature and calm amid the clamor of an urban sprawl, Rosetta Getty's home echoes the contrasts and contradictions of LA. "I love the variety of this city and this house," she says. "It has a combined sense of past and present that I feel reflects our world."

MARINA LAMBTON

Marina Lambton first visited Villa Cetinale when she was ten years old. "We came as a family to have lunch with Tony Lambton, and my first memory is the pack of fifteen terrifying dogs barking at the gate," she recalls.

Barking dogs are not the typical beginning to a romance, but two decades on, Marina is now married to Tony's son, Ned, and chatelaine of the historic Tuscan villa, running it both as a private family home and overseeing its rental to the fortunate few.

The villa has a fascinating past. It was built by architect Carlo Fontana in 1680 for Cardinal Flavio Chigi, the nephew of Pope Alexander VII, and remained in the Chigi family for the next 300 years, hosting the Palio horse race seven times and enjoying a visit from Napoleon Bonaparte in 1811. In 1978 it was bought by Ned's father, Lord Lambton, a former MP whose political career had been derailed by scandal. He decamped to Cetinale with his partner, Claire Ward, and lived there for the rest of his life, creating one of Tuscany's most beautiful gardens while hosting riotous parties for the likes of Princess Margaret and Mick Jagger.

Today, things at Cetinale are a little less riotous and a lot more comfortable. In 2011 Ned and Marina undertook a comprehensive overhaul of the villa that included putting on a brand-new roof, installing 6,500 meters of new pipes, adding much-needed bathrooms, and refinishing nearly 10,000 meters of walls and ceilings.

The huge project was managed by Camilla Guinness, who was a great friend of Tony's and whose own house, Arniano, is nearby. "I arrived on the scene just as the restoration was getting underway, when the villa was totally gutted and all the furniture was in storage," says Marina. "Thank God for Camilla. She understands the place so well so she was the perfect person to do the job. We totally trusted everything she did, and of course it was absolutely amazing."

The refurbishment returned the thirteen-bedroom house to its former glory. "It now feels very clean and fresh, not crumbling at all," says Marina.

Walls were repainted, frescoes restored, and the fabric on chairs and beds refreshed. The odd modern touches here and there, such as huge stand-alone bathtubs, have added an edge of contemporary luxury, but otherwise the house has retained the inimitable atmosphere that both the Chigis and Tony Lambton would have recognized. There have even been some new discoveries. When a fire broke out in the sitting room on the piano nobile, it revealed

a painting on the ceiling that had been hidden for centuries under a layer of white paint. With the house now home to the couple's three young children, Stella, Claud, and Acony Belle, as well as hosting groups of paying guests throughout the year, it requires constant maintenance. "Things get damaged quite often," Marina says. "I have to get things repaired or reupholstered. It's a question of constant sourcing of furniture, lights, material. It's really fun."

At Cetinale, the outside is just as much the star as the inside. Dotted with statues by the seventeenth-century sculptor Giuseppe Mazzuoli, as well as a number of votive chapels decorated in fading frescoes and the five-story Romitorio, the villa's grounds are a cacophony of cypress-lined avenues, formal topiary gardens, and romantically tangled woodland. Entering the shadows of the walled Holy Wood—known as the Thebaid—feels like walking into the pages of a fairy tale. Rustling indicates the presence of wild boar and deer, and it was here that Lord Lambton came across a bas-relief depicting a visit by Cosimo de' Medici, which now sits in the wall of the dining room.

The grounds were the source for some of Lord Lambton's infamous ghost stories, which he liked to recount to his guests before they made the long walk to their bedrooms. Marina laughs: "He had a wicked sense of humor and loved trying to spook people. Apparently there is a ghost in the well by the monastery and also a murderous cardinal in the house, but I've never seen them. To me, Cetinale is the least spooky place."

AUTHOR BIOGRAPHIES

Alex Eagle is a globally recognized creative director who has revolutionized retail through her two concept spaces: Alex Eagle Studio and The Store. Expanding the remit beyond shopping to incorporate fashion, art, publishing, culture, food, philanthropy, and interiors, Eagle has forged relationships with a cross section of creatives across all disciplines and from around the world, cultivating a new ethos of collaboration and innovation that extends from art exhibitions and restaurants to bespoke tailoring, clothes design, and antique and contemporary furniture. She has been instrumental in the creation of a new cultural hub at 180 the Strand. She lives in London with her husband, son, daughter, and two step-daughters. *More Than Just A House* is her first book.

Kate Martin is an internationally renowned photographer. Arriving in the UK from New Zealand, she started her career taking pictures in the music industry before expanding into fashion and interiors. Her photographs have featured in *Vogue, Vanity Fair, Architectural Digest, How To Spend It,* and *W* magazine among others, while her portraits of actors, artists, musicians, designers, and tastemakers have appeared in publications around the world. She lives in London with her husband and daughter. *More Than Just A House* is her third book.

Tish Wrigley is a writer with nearly a decade's experience in art, fashion, and culture. She was assistant editor at *AnOther* magazine and AnOthermag.com and is now contributing editor at The Spaces. Her work has appeared in *FT Life & Arts,* CNN Style, and Alex Eagle Studio Journal. She lives in London. *More Than Just A House* is her first book.